BURREN VILLAGES

BURREN VILLAGES

TALES OF HISTORY AND IMAGINATION

COMPILED & EDITED BY

SARAH POYNTZ

MERCIER PRESS

IRISH PUBLISHER – IRISH STORY

MERCIER PRESS

Cork

www.mercierpress.ie

Trade enquiries to CMD BookSource,
55a Spruce Avenue, Stillorgan Industrial Park,
Blackrock, County Dublin

ISBN: 978 1 85635 674 9

10 9 8 7 6 5 4 3 2 1

A CIP record for this title is available from the British Library

Printed and bound in the EU.

Contents

To the people of the Burren coastal villages
with thanks and affection

Preface

Fintan O'Toole

'Every place,' writes Rebecca Solnit in *A Book of Migrations*, 'exists in two versions, as an exotic and a local. The exotic is a casual acquaintance who must win hearts through charm and beauty and sites of historical interest, but the local is made up of the accretion of individual memory and sustenance, the

Aerial view of the Burren Coast
© Redmond's of Roscrea

maternal landscape of uneventful routine. The Burren seemed to be an old local place that was becoming almost exclusively exotic.'

It's not true, of course, that the Burren and the coastal villages dotted around its edges are exclusively exotic. They are places like any other, places of uneventful routine, of economic activity and political conflict, of the struggle to survive and of human affections and disaffections. But it is hard to deny that these mundane aspects of life unfold in an extraordinary landscape. The daily life of the local villages is embedded within a location that cannot resist the exotic. For a very long time now, the Burren has been an imagined place as well as a real one. It attracts the gaze of outsiders, who project onto it their own desires and meanings. This impulse is not to be dismissed as mere wish-fulfilment, but neither should it obscure the sense in which this place is a community as well as a landscape, a locality that is human as well as natural. The outsider's gaze can be ignorant of the social realities of the place. It can try to turn the Burren into a timeless space in which real human life is at best an intrusion, at worst impertinence. But if it avoids that temptation, it can also provide the imaginative context in which the local can be seen as something more than mundane.

The paradox of the Burren is that no landscape is more obviously human and yet none has been more dehumanised. We know, from the density of ancient archaeological sites, that this has been a place of human settlement for thousands of years. We know that the landscape itself, its famously stark aspect of skeletal limestone, is at least in part a product of human activity in cutting trees and causing erosion of topsoil. We know, thanks to the pioneering work of Brendan Dunford, co-founder of Burrenbeo, that the very profusion of nature in the Burren, the fabulous diversity of its flora, is utterly dependent on specific farming practices and that there is therefore no clear line of separation between the human and natural worlds. Knowing all of this, the long-established tendency to see the Burren as a purely natural, timeless landscape is all the more remarkable.

Consider, for example, the quotation that turns up in virtually every discussion of the Burren, from the memoirs of the Cromwellian General Edmund Ludlow: 'After two days' march, without anything remarkable but bad quarters, we entered into the Barony of Burren, of which it is said that it is a country where there is not water enough to drown a man, wood enough to hang one, not earth enough to bury him; which last is so scarce that the inhabitants steal it from one another.' Ludlow's grimly violent description seems to sum up the idea of the Burren as an inhuman place, a landscape that cannot sustain human death, let alone human life. What is interesting, however, is that Ludlow's musings on the Burren do not stop there. Almost no one quotes the immediate continuation of his memoir: 'and yet their cattle are very fat; for the grass growing in the tufts of earth, of two or three foot square, that lie beneath the rocks, which are of limestone, is very sweet and nourishing'. Ludlow is not in fact endorsing the idea of the Burren as a bleak inhuman landscape at all. The first bit of the quotation is itself a quotation ('it is said'). The second part is more of a direct observation, and one that contradicts the first. Ludlow is in fact exploring a paradox: this place is not quite what it is reputed to be. It is bleak on the surface and bountiful beneath. It is a complicated, contradictory place of scarce soil and fat cattle, of scarce water and sweet grass.

This contradiction, moreover, points to one of the ways in which the Burren is such a fertile ground for imaginings. It can be thought of in contradictory ways. One of the simplest of these contradictions is that between bleakness and bounty.

In the medieval chronicle, *Leabhar na gCeart,* we read of 'ten hundred oxen from Borinn' being part of the tributes of Cashel to the kings of Erin. Geoffrey Keating tells us in turn that 'the King of Cashel or Munster received a yearly tribute of 1,000 bullocks, 1,000 cows, 1,000 weathers, and 1000 cloaks' from the inhabitants of the Burren. This suggests that the Burren has long been a highly productive landscape, occupied by people who knew how to use it to sustain them and to sustain it in order that it might do so. The idea of the flowering rock, contained in the very name of Corcomroe Abbey (*Sancta Maria de Petra Fertilis*) is an embodied paradox. But it is also an obvious source of pride and wonder. It suggests that there is not a necessary contradiction between the economic and magical aspects of this landscape. The production of bounty from this rocky domain *is* a kind of magic.

Yet side by side with this idea of the Burren as a place of abundant life, there is also the idea of it being a landscape of death. This is present, of course, in Ludlow's imagery of hanging, drowning and burying. But in more recent times, one of the ways in which the human impact on the landscape is occluded is to make the Burren a post-apocalyptic landscape, imbued with death. Consider Brian Walters in *Fallen: My travels in Ireland and Eastern Europe:* 'On first glance, the Burren looks like a graveyard of tightly packed tombstones'. Equally, Rebecca Solnit in *A Book of Migrations* writes that 'the Burren on this stormy day seemed like an abandoned landscape, like the surface of a planet whose inhabitants had all vanished an indeterminate time ago. No cars, almost no birds, and signs of cattle in the fields but no cows, just a flat, rocky expanse to the horizon, scoured and gnawed by wind and rain – nothing but botany, geology, meteorology, and ruins ... Even the whitethorn trees seemed lonely, each set at a distance from the next along the walls.' W. B. Yeats at the start of his play *The Dreaming of the Bones*, which is set at Corcomroe, emphasises this same loneliness – the word lonely or loneliness occurs three times in the first speech. The stones of the Burren are haunted: 'For certain days the stones where you must lie / Have in the hour before the break of day / Been haunted.' Yet this deathliness, this haunted landscape, also stirs uneasily. Musicians describe the Burren as a place in which life and death, the real and the fantastical, the waking and the dreamlike, are entwined:

> Have not old writers said
> That dizzy dreams can spring
> From the dry bones of the dead?

Again, we find this idea of a place that refuses to be fixed in the imagination. Just as Ludlow's land of death and destitution suddenly becomes a place of fat cattle and sweet grass, Yeats' dry bones of the dead are in fact a spring from which dizzy dreams can gush. Bleakly desolate one moment and fruitfully productive the next, an abandoned planet and a spring of dreams, the place seems both to shape itself to the moods of the viewer and to make those moods unstable to the point of absolute contradiction. Just as the light of the Burren seems liquid in its inconstancy, so the imaginative light that is cast upon the place seems to reflect the same habit of endless flux. It is fascinating to trace this fluidity even in the most sober and official descriptions of the place. Here is *The Parliamentary Gazetteer of Ireland of 1846* seeking a dry description of the Burren:

> The general features of the greater part of the Barony of Burrin [*sic*] are altogether different from those of any other part of the country. In the central portion of this district, the entire surface seems one unbroken mass of limestone rock; and the bare hills, rising from the shore to a great elevation, in regularly receding terraced flights, present a vast amphitheatrical outline. The disjointed blocks, composing the surface of this immense concavity ... are laid generally in horizontal lines, giving to the whole, at a distance, a regular and formal character. The more elevated parts are destitute of herbage, and present to the eye an arid, cold and joyless waste, unchanged by either summer's sun or winter's cold, and but little varied by either light or shade. Yet the upland grounds, though extremely rocky, produce a short sweet herbage, and annually nourish great numbers of sheep for the great fair at Ballinasloe.

Within this passage, we find a range of unstable contradictions. The landscape is barren ('arid, cold and joyless waste') and bountiful (that sweet grass again). It is foreign to the point of being not really Irish ('altogether different'), yet it is also part of the ordinary local economy ('the great fair at Ballinasloe'). It is entirely natural ('one unbroken mass of limestone rock') yet also artificial, the landscape 'amphitheatrical', 'regular and formal', as if laid out by a giant human architect.

The capacity of the Burren to appear very different to different viewers can be summed up in the contrast between the *Gazetteer*'s description of the uplands as 'unchanged by either summer's sun or winter's cold, and but little varied by either light or shade' and the description of the Burren by

Emily Lawless in her novel *Hurrish*: 'it presents to the eye a succession of low hills, singularly grey in tone – deepening often, towards evening, into violet or dull reddish plum colour – sometimes, after sunset, to a pale ghostly iridescence.'

Yet, if Lawless' description seems much more accurate to contemporary lovers of the Burren, it should not be assumed that she saw it as a place of beauty. The very idea that this landscape is beautiful and exotic is not inherent within the place but is a product of perception, and thus of imagination. In the same novel, *Hurrish*, written in 1886 as a kind of riposte to nationalist novels like Charles Kickham's *Knocknagow*, and read by the then prime minister, Gladstone, as a source of enlightenment on Irish problems, Lawless is quite clear that the Burren is not a beautiful landscape. The opening line is, 'Wilder regions there are few to be found, even in the wildest west of Ireland, than that portion of North Clare known to its inhabitants as "The Burren" ...' This might seem to be the prelude to an evocation of wild and romantic beauty, calculated to appeal to a metropolitan audience, but Lawless goes on explicitly to disavow any such possibility: 'The Burren is not – in all probability never will be – a tourist-haunt, but for the few who know it, it is a place apart, a distinct personality – strange, remote, indescribable.' She regards the landscape with horror: 'Here and there over the top and sides of the drift a little thin grass has spread itself, through which trenches have been torn, showing the earth and stones below. Truly a grim scene! – suggestive of nothing so much as one of those ugly little early German prints, where every stick and stone seems to be grimacing with unpleasant intention.' Here again, we see the tensions and contradictions in attempts to describe the place. It is on the one hand wild but on the other suggestive of a German print. It is aesthetic and unique ('a place apart') but ugly and hostile.

Within this set of tensions and contradictions, however, there is one constant – an anthropomorphic impulse to read an emotional bleakness into the Burren landscape. This extends even into scientific literature. Edward Dillon Mapother, in *The Treatment of Chronic Skin Diseases, With an Appendix of Lisdoonvarna Spas* (1872), manages to get a sense of desolation even into an account of the curative properties of the spa waters: 'The Burren Mountains, and the countless acres of flat stones, mapped, however, into fields, are not surpassed in bleakness by any in the world ...' And here is J. R. Kilroe in *A Description of the Soil-Geology of Ireland*: 'The Burren district of Clare is notable for scenery of a peculiar character, unique to Ireland. Wide stretches of bare limestone there prevail, trenched with gaping crevices, deep gorges, and valleys separating terraced hills, the pseudo-artificial appearance of which, combined with an unusual sterility of the region, impresses the beholder with a sense of weird desolateness.'

This sense of desolation became, over time, so strongly entrenched that it could co-exist even with a vivid sense of the lively sociability of the Burren villages. The American poet Ben Howard, wrote 'The Holy Alls' in the Burren in 1950, describing himself as:

> The Yank who lives alone in Ballyvaughan
> And sometimes can be found in Connor's pub
> Sipping his whiskies with the best of them –

But this image of sociability is undercut by his figuring of what he calls 'the most intransigent of landscapes':

A coastal stretch comprised of creviced rock.
A boulder meadow, someone might have called it,
Were not its contours quite the opposite
Of anything hospitable or kind
To lost sheep or ramblers like myself.
Conjure, if you will, a sandless desert
In tones of grey, its western edge converging
With bands of shifting, pewter cumuli,
Its eastern border reaching out to sea.
Within the cavities between the rocks
The colonies of violet lobelia
Sent up their quiet message of survival,
As if to contradict a larger voice
Which spoke of poverty and stark extinction.

Which place, you wonder, does he inhabit? The Ballyvaughan where he can drink whiskey with the rest or the coastal stretch that is the 'opposite of anything hospitable or kind'? The 'sandless desert' or the landscape that teems with violet lobelias?

These tensions in the representation of the Burren crystallise around a stark question – is it Irish or not? The question may seem ridiculous but the fact is that the Burren and its people have been represented as both non-Irish and ultra-Irish, both some kind of foreign, detached tribe and the very essence of the nation. John Betjeman begins his poem 'Ireland With Emily' with the line, 'Stony seaboard, far and foreign'. In Lawless' *Hurrish*, the Burren man of the title is given an exotic tinge: 'Irish in every feature, look, and gesture, there was yet a smack of something foreign about him, to be accounted for possibly by that oft-quoted admixture of Spanish blood, the result of bygone centuries of more or less continuous intercourse.' Of

Hurrish's mother, Lawless writes: 'In Bridget O'Brien the southern type was also strongly visible. Women like her – as gaunt, as wrinkled, as black-browed, as witch-like – may be seen seated upon thousands of doorsteps all over the Spanish peninsula.' The Burren is thus a far-flung province of Spanish exoticism.

By a small stretch of the imagination, this idea of foreignness morphs into a positive otherworldliness. David A. Wilson writes in *Ireland, A Bicycle and a Tin Whistle* (1995) of 'the Burren, a wilderness of limestone, where otherworlds collide and combine'. This notion of the Burren as some kind of meeting place between this world and the next is deeply rooted. We find Lady Gregory, in *The Bogie Man*, writing of Taig and Darby, who are emigrating to America to work as steeplejacks. Darby proclaims, 'what signifies chimneys? We'll go up in them till we'll take a view of the Seven Stars! It is out beyond the hills of Burren I will cast my eye, till I see the gates of Heaven!'

Yet, at the same time as the place and its people are seen as suspiciously foreign or exotically otherworldly, the Burren can also be seen as a touchstone of quintessential Irishness. Lady Gregory herself writes, in *The Kiltartan Poetry Book,* of the very sight of the Burren hills as a spur to patriotic identification with Ireland: 'For a romantic love of country had awakened in me, perhaps through the wild beauty of my home, from whose hillsides I could see the mountains of Burren and Iar Connacht …' George Moore actually claimed, in his autobiographical *Ave*, to have seen, during a visit to the Burren, what he believed to be an emanation of the female spirit of Ireland, Cathleen Ní Houlihan.

A little less fancifully, W. B. Yeats came to see the colours and contours of the Burren as a possible grounding for a distinctively Irish visual art. He wrote in 'Ireland and the Arts': 'Even the landscape painter, who paints a place he loves, and that no other man has painted, soon discovers that no style learned in the studios is wholly fitted to his purpose. And I cannot but believe that if our painters of highland cattle and moss-covered barns were to care enough for their country to care for what makes it different from other countries, they would discover, when struggling, it may be, to paint the exact grey of the bare Burren Hills, and of a sudden, it may be a new style, their very selves. And I admit though in this I am moved by some touch of fanaticism, that even when I see an old subject written or painted in a new way, I am yet jealous for Cuchulain, and for Baile an Ailinn, and for those grey mountains that are still lacking their celebration.'

Given all of these simultaneous versions of the Burren as desolate and bountiful, romantic and ugly, natural and artificial, foreign and essentially Irish, how can the actual lives of its people be understood? The answer all too often has been to imagine them as simply part of the landscape, and thus as existing outside of history. There is a sense of timelessness that robs people of their lived experience of change, conflict and renewal. One way of removing people from history is to make them animals. In Lawless' description of Hurrish's mother, she is linked with a dark and dangerous animality. Bridget is compared to 'an elderly bird of prey – a vulture, old, yet with claws ever upon the watch to tear and a beak which yearns to plunge itself into the still palpitating flesh. Her eyes were black – a wicked black …' More humanely Rebecca Solnit evokes a sense of archaeological time in her descriptions of the Burren, in which the real, ordinary time frame of Burren communities seems to disappear: 'In the daytime, it seemed possible to believe that human beings were rare, solitary creatures who existed largely to rearrange the stone according to slow passing fashions into tombs, stone forts, churches, walls, and that there was no other scale of time but the aeons of geological formation and erosion, the millennia of architectural styles, the decades of building, and the hourly shifts of clouds and wind and rain ... of all places I visited, the Burren felt loneliest for its abandonment.'

This sense that the Burren unfolds according to a different, and inhuman, timescale, feeds into a notion of the people who actually live in the place as some kind of throwback to a distant era. Again Lawless in *Hurrish* is striking in this regard: 'Everything that the eye rests on tells us that we are on one of the last standpoints of an old world, worn out with its own profusion, and reduced here to the barest elements. Mother earth, once young, buxom, frolicsome, is here a wrinkled woman, sitting alone in the evening of her days, and looking with melancholy eyes at the sunset.' James Plunkett in *The Gems She Wore* writes, 'Inland lies the Burren country. It too seems to belong to another age ...' Betjeman, in 'Ireland with Emily', moves from the stones that he sees to the notion that the people, too, are Stone Age:

> Stone-walled cabins thatched with reeds,
> Where a Stone Age people breeds
> The last of Europe's stone age race.

This anthropological attitude is satisfied by Samuel Beckett in his novel *Watt*, in which the ne'er-do-well student Mr Ernest Louit has to justify the use of his grant before a college committee. He produces for the committee 'an old man dressed in kilt, plaid, brogues, and, in spite of the cold, a pair of silk socks made fast to the purple calves by an unpretentious pair of narrow mauve suspenders, and holding a large black felt hat under his arm. Louit said, "This, gentlemen, is Mr Thomas Louit Nackybal, native of Burren. There he has spent all his life, thence he was loath to remove, thither he longs to return, to kill his pig, his solitary perennial companion."' Of his mental capacities, Louit insists that apart from the 'dumbly flickering' knowledge of 'how to extract, from the ancestral half-acre of moraine, the maximum of nourishment, for himself and his pig, with the minimum of labour, all, I am convinced, is an ecstasy of darkness and silence'. (We later discover that Mr Nackybal is not what he seems. He is really called Tiser and lives in a room near the canal in Dublin.)

In writing about the Burren now the task is not necessarily to disentangle all the contradictions and paradoxes. In a sense, those starkly different perceptions, so often contained within the same description, are testaments to the richness of the place. It is indeed deeply textured and many layered. It is also physically fluid, caught between mountain and sea, light and shadow, the stark and the profuse. Its bare rock can act as a giant screen on which people project their own yearnings. That is partly why it inspires imaginative responses and those responses in turn have shaped our notion of the place. None of us can entirely avoid seeing it through the accumulated perceptions of all those who have looked before.

The task, rather, is to remember that the people who live in the Burren are not timeless outgrowths of the landscape. On the contrary, it is they who have, over the millennia, shaped it and nurtured it, drawn from it and given back to it. There is no clear line between the natural and human aspects of the place, or between the physical and imaginative ones. Unless the Burren is able to sustain its people, it will not itself be sustained, but will return to scrub. Unless it is able to inspire emotions, ideas and images, the spiritual energy needed to cherish and protect its richness will not be available. Placing the people back at the heart of the Burren does not diminish all the ways in which that landscape transcends the human. It enhances the crucial awareness that the place has its people and the people have their place within it.

From the Rine to Corcomroe

Tony Hartnett

There is something here that pulls at you inside. It's like an image from childhood that skims just below the surface of memory from time to time, wanting you to remember but never staying long enough to let you. You have a need for acceptance, to feel 'part of'. And you feel part of here, with all its unquestioning ruggedness and undemanding beauty, its fleeting moments and endless seasons that paint your thoughts with light. You visit and absorb the memory of rock and water and watery air, the energy of earth bursting with a rainbow of spring colour, carpeting the mountainy meadows. The salt-scented air finds refuge in your breath, your pores, your very soul and, even without knowing, becomes part of what you are. It echoes the infinite inside you, that time in silent moments when you break free from the shackles of broken dreams and rise to feed what life has left malnourished. The sea sweeps in on burnished sand to coat your naked feet with its deep scents, swirling sun-warmed weed like a lover's embrace around you. The grey-rock hills, tinged rose in the setting sun, are a prayer to a cloudless sky.

At Bishop's Quarter, ancient dry-stone walls rise from

under dunes like slumbering dinosaurs, their ridged backs breaking sand. You gaze and picture the leathery, blistered hands that built them, stone by stone, long before your father drew breath. A division of land that became a division of time. Built, buried, reborn, mute reminders of hardier men and the brevity of life. Yards away the cliff, pock-marked and crumbling, inches further back in the face of the sea's changing moods. The swifts make homes here, darting in and out like black arrows on summer evenings. On the grassy ledge above, clusters of spring gentian, as blue as God would have wanted, vie with buttery primrose to catch the sun's last rays.

The sand between the rocks and rock pools is littered with the prints of foraging sea birds. Oystercatchers and curlews, gulls and sandpipers stay year round. Winter brings Brent geese and great northern divers in large numbers, where they bob on choppy seas, aloof, well-travelled, noisy. Behind the car park, at the edge of the little lake that's fed and drained by the sea every day, stands a solitary, snow-white egret, as silent and still as journey's end.

On summer days this place hums with life but only when it is still does it speak. The silvery green marram grasses wave in sinewy, sensual whispers of air, as seductive as dancers in love. The shore lark, suspended in the blue above, will break your heart in song. The sea will steal away the pieces and keep them for herself.

In Corcomroe Abbey, you trace the steps of holy men, your footsteps echoing on hallowed walls. You hear them sing at evening's end, chanting air-dressed prayers from ragged books clasped in death-pale hands. Their songs still linger here, part of the fabric of stone and resting place: songs of repentance and absolution, of Christian passion and burning hearts.

You trace the letters carved in stone beneath your feet 400 years ago. The graves of men who loved women in a place where women never loved. Men of God lie under grassy mounds, their spirits still here, their eyes fixed on the infinite. Rooks nest high in the roofless walls, swallows shoot through glassless windows like souls in search of a host.

When a soft, misty rain sweeps in from the sea you stand here, face upturned, eyes closed and listen to the fullness of silence. This is a place of stillness, of effigies of bishops cast in stone and locked in time. A place of retreat from all noise but the noise of thought, a womb within a cloister within a fragment of time. It is a place where you revert to the essence of your spirit-home.

A thousand years have come and gone. The walls still stand; the living come to pray for the dead, when it is the living who need the prayers. On the snows of winter and the blossoming of summer the kestrel's circling shadow falls. Death is suspended in the rush to complete the circle of life.

The mountaintops that overlook the sea across to Connemara's Twelve Pins are rocky fountains of pure colour. In spring and summer, the mossy earth gives birth to orchids and avens, gentians and cranesbills, ferns and meadow grasses. A tapestry of all that earth and heaven, in secret harmony, can weave. You stand here sometimes in the heat of a summer's day and remember how you lay nearby in a tiny field with your lover, blinded by a searing sun. You remember the warmth of her hand in yours, the ceaseless buzzing of insects and the sharpness of the grasses behind your head. You travelled together to a place high above where you lay, two kites entwined against the blue.

The dead are here too. Great mounds of limestone are tombs where sleeping queens still watch over all they loved.

For what greater love can you have for the soil that gave you life than to flow back into it. To become what you are when you are no more.

Wild mountain goats roam the paths and craggy rock, moving from place to place like a streaming cloud of misty incense. Time has forgotten them. The king among them stands on a rocky ledge, a lone silhouette against a fading light, and in his silence affirms his own importance. Where he will lead, the others will follow, until weakness of age will cast him from the herd, dethroned by some new pretender and abandoned to his fate.

The sand on the Rine is as white as old Jamaica's. It sifts through your fingers like powder, a million years of shell and rock pouring from your hand. The sea that caresses the horseshoe beach is pale turquoise and cinnabar green, deep blue and slate grey, a mirror to the moody sky. Gleninagh Castle, haunted by memories of darker days and stony home to birds of prey, is a silent sentinel. You cross the fields to touch its face and again remember another time here, when you were loved and you loved, and you spent a restless night under a yellowing moon.

Across the bay, a Martello tower that Joyce might have peopled with Mulligans from Clare, is a beautiful shape. Sensual in any light, its graceful curves are a contrast to Gleninagh Castle's boxy posture. The blackthorn trees are sooty fingers against the sky. Wind-bent, they point inland as though to warn you away from the sea – the focal point of so many childhood memories where laughter rang in a warm, infectious cascade of unrestrained joy. It pounds against the rock here like an endless heartbeat, taking what it pleases but giving in return. The sea is memory, the cold umbilical cord that won't be severed.

The trails and paths that wind like grey ribbons across the hills are a journey through time. You walk them to be alone with your demons or your angels. Wedge tombs and dolmens, a startled hare bounding across the crevices of limestone rock, a fox curled up in the thicket of bracken. You leap a dry-stone wall, the early morning sun at your back, and lose yourself between light and shade. Far below, a summer fog not yet burned by the rising sun drapes itself like gossamer over sleeping houses and a jigsaw of fields, hangs like an unused blanket down the slopes of Cappanawalla. You rest on a ledge of furrowed limestone, your shadow long on the dewy grass, and melt into the first warmth of an early summer's day.

On Bishop's Quarter beach you take your kite to the air, watching it drift lazily above your head. Currents lift it high into the sun, parting the clouds. Between you and it, a simple length of string. The wind takes it, pulling it away, free of you and the dreary earth. Your heart soars and breaks, all at once, as you watch it fly, singing in the wind. Further and further, higher and higher, until all that remains is a memory of what was briefly yours, a song that rings in the hollow where she once lay.

A Little History

Sarah Poyntz & Jim Hyland

The villages of Ballyvaughan, Bell Harbour, Ucht Máma, Gleninagh and Fanore, in the long history of the region where they lie, the Burren of north-west County Clare, are very recent dots on its landscape. The word 'Burren' comes from the Irish and means 'rocky place'. This place extends inland for

Ballyvaughan from the sea
© Karin Funke

28

about 350 square kilometres from the Atlantic coast. Today it is one of the great karst landscapes of the world but it was formed over 300 million years ago by small sea organisms, layer by limestone layer. We can stand on its expanse of calcareous pavements or clints, gaze on its fissures or grykes stretching out from land to sea, from valley to mountain top, and recall its antiquity: 25,000 years ago the moving glaciers of the Ice Age helped to smooth, to round the rocks that wind, rain and salt coming from the ocean had weathered, shaping the limestone into the Burren that we know in this second millennium. While we read these words, this process is still going on.

The Burren is one of nature's great drainage systems. Its limestone, being porous, enables accumulations of rainwater to seep through and down into its underground caves, tunnels and rivers. Its mild Atlantic climate promotes its flora, its unique combination of Arctic, Mediterranean and native wild flowers.

Millions of years of slow, gradual change have resulted in this beauty, a beauty that touches the heart, the mind, taming them into wonder, into quiet joy, into the peace of stillness. Yet the bare hills that most people exclaim about when they first see the Burren, this almost treeless land, are the result of bad farming practices by ancient settlers when the original trees were cut and the soil, because rootless, eroded rapidly.

When therefore do the villages enter this picture? The answer is well over hundreds of millions years after the limestone layers were formed. The man who knows every clint, every cranny of this wonderland of karst, who has lived in it as boy and man, local historian Jim Hyland, is the person to share with us his knowledge of the area's history.

An Outline of the Area
Jim Hyland

Just as the past, distant and recent, plays a part in each human life, so too it has its role in the life of the community, in the very place we inhabit, where we live. It is so with the Burren coastal villages. Of course their history stretches far into the past, a lot further than the individual's chronicle. All around us, we see the history made by our predecessors in this region. Their remains, beginning over 4,000 years ago, dolmens, wedge tombs, cairns, fulachtaí fia (ancient cooking sites), forts, castle keeps, churches, lie near us. The great dolmen of Poulnabrone was the final resting place of twenty-eight people, both adults and children.

Gaelic culture is evident in the remains of Bardic and Brehon Law sites, the former at Finavarra, the latter at Cathair Mhic Neachtain, the O'Davoren Law School. To stand near the Bardic site is to remember how seriously the Gaels took their poetry and oratory, seen in the length of their poetic apprenticeship, how the word of a bard could ruin a chieftain in those days. To gaze at the Brehon Law School ruins is to admire the place given to women in its structured and practical legal system. To ramble around the Gaelic/Celtic churches is to be struck by their simplicity.

The three little churches at Ucht Máma or Oughtmama, near Bell Harbour, built during the Gaelic period (twelfth century) are wonderful examples of these simple places of worship with their delightful carvings. Yeats spoke of 'grey Oughtmama' and it can be grey, but when the sun shines, it is burnished to gold. It snuggles into the side of Turlough Hill close to the traces of terracing and its millstream was worked by the clergy long before Rome established its rules and regulations in the island. It seems isolated now but probably was not so in its heyday when people walked everywhere. It preceded Cistercian Corcomroe nearby, which dates from the Norman period, twelfth to thirteenth centuries. Dónal Mór O'Brien probably founded this church – he died in 1194 – although there is confusion about its founder and indeed precise dates. What is straightforward is that the Cistercian monks built this abbey and called it *Petra Fertilis* (the Fertile Rock). The Cistercians were very knowledgeable farmers and came to this valley finding it well watered (there were at least five wells in this townland). They worked a land that might not

Twelfth-century churches, Ucht Máma, before 1914
© Lawrence Collection, Courtesy of the National Library of Ireland

have had deep topsoil but which was fertile, as it still is today. The carvings in this ruin are fine, very delicate and are of the flowers found in the surrounding Burren.

The new invaders, the Normans, were not threatening to the old Gaelic customs because they readily adopted them. However, with their introduction of the Cistercians and the foundation of Corcomroe and other monasteries throughout the island, the rule of Rome became well established in Ireland and saw the demise of the old Celtic Christianity. The Normans were followed by other waves of invaders, such as the Elizabethans in the sixteenth century and the Cromwellians in the seventeenth. With the dissolution of Corcomroe and of all Irish abbeys and monasteries, under Henry VIII of England, the old monastic way of life gradually faded and English rule began to spread throughout the country, leaving us with beautiful ecclesiastical ruins.

Today the centuries-old stories of both Ucht Máma and Corcomroe still circulate. One story is that St Colman of Aran founded Ucht Máma. He is said to have fallen out with the people of Aran, left the islands and arrived at Ucht Máma, swearing that never again did he wish to hear or see a man from Aran. One day at Ucht Máma he heard the bells of Aran. He immediately departed and ended up at Killmacduagh, a monastic settlement near Gort, County Galway.

Close to both Ucht Máma and Corcomroe is the famous Corker Pass, known to the local people as Bothar na Mias (the Road of the Dishes). Legend has it that on Easter Sunday, having fasted severely throughout Lent, St Colman and his servant prayed for food. At that moment St Colman's brother, King Guaire, was feasting in his castle at Kinvara. Suddenly all the dishes rose from the tables, flew out through the door and kept flying up the pass until they reached St Colman's sanctuary. Guaire's horse soldiers followed them and, as they approached, the horses' hooves became stuck and they could go no further. It is said that the servant ate so much that he died!

Our Burren and its later coastal villages are rich in old, mainly ruined, castle keeps. Gleninagh Castle stands by one of the many holy wells of the area. Bell Harbour, Muckinish, Fanore and Ballyvaughan all have castle remains, but Ballyvaughan has two restored castle keeps, that of Newtown, renovated by Mary Hawkes Greene and her late husband, Michael Greene, and Gregan Castle restored by Brian and Anna Hussey. Newtown is now part of the Burren College of Art, while Gregan Castle is a private home but is open to the public on certain days of the year. Of Ballyvaughan Castle, sited near the edge of the harbour, very little remains. Here the O'Loghlens held sway.[1]

The region, like the rest of Ireland, was subjected to English laws and had the same rebellions, almost one rebellion each half century. It was under an English administration in the nineteenth century that the villages came into being. The fishing industry and the produce from the fertile land were largely responsible for their establishment. The construction of piers at Ballyvaughan, Bell Harbour and Gleninagh boosted their ability to supply food for sale to neighbouring towns. The piers and small harbours were constructed with financial help from the local landlords and the fisheries board. This encouraged the turf boats to ply from Galway and Connemara with their well-hidden bottles of poitín to the small harbours.

---

1   There are a number of spellings of the family name common in the area: O'Loghlen, O'Loughlin, O'Lochlen and O'Lochlainn. The original spellings are used throughout.

Ballyvaughan had two piers, the Old Pier (1829) and the New Pier (1837), still known by these names today.

The landlord of Ballyvaughan also provided a boat to enable farmers and merchants to send goods to and from the big markets in Galway. Events outside Ireland also played a part in what became an improved life for some people in the village; the Napoleonic Wars between France and England resulted in England's increased need for food, so agricultural produce and fish were exported there.

The population increased in the villages, with Ballyvaughan becoming the principal village nearest to the Clare/Galway border. By 1835, its population had grown to 235 with 35 houses. Not everyone became prosperous and a workhouse was built in 1841 to cater for the destitute and for girls who became pregnant outside of marriage, as the girl's relatives would often disown her. A primary school within the workhouse was provided for these children.

The 1840s brought the years of famine, culminating in the Great Famine of 1845–1849. The coastal villages were slightly better off than those inland because of their proximity to the sea and the availability of fish and shellfish. The deserted villages with their ruined cottages, as well as ruins in Fanore, Gleninagh to Ballyvaughan and Bell Harbour, are reminders of days of terrible sadness, death and unending heartbreak. It also brought the separation of emigration, when people took ships to the United States, Canada, Australia, England and Argentina. Many landlords used the catastrophe of the Great Famine to evict their tenants. According to Robert Kee in *The Most Distressful Country*, 'Over a hundred thousand persons had been officially evicted from their holdings in 1849.'

In 1850, the Ballyvaughan Union was established and

became an administrative centre for the village and surrounding parishes. It was responsible for the upkeep of roads, health and water services. In 1854, the first primary school for 200 pupils opened in Ballyvaughan. The nineteenth century was also the century of church building throughout the country, and 1860 saw the completion of Ballyvaughan Roman Catholic church as Irish immigrants in Australia made a collection and sent £2,000 for the building. Its construction was delayed by the collapse of the belfry in a storm, but the local landlord (the Duke of Buckingham) donated £200 towards a new belfry. Fanore and the church at New Quay, which served Bell Harbour, were also built. At this time the parishes of Gleninagh, Drumcreehy and Rathborney were amalgamated into the parish of Ballyvaughan.

In the mid 1860s, Lord Annally purchased the lands owned by Buckingham and he appointed an agent, William Lane Joynt, a Dublin lawyer. He resided in the newly built Clareville House. Colonel Whyte, who succeeded Lord Annally but who lived in County Tipperary, agreed with Lane Joynt, that the village needed a proper water supply. A reservoir, fed by mountain springs, was constructed about five kilometres from the village. Pipes were laid to the townlands and Ballyvaughan union was responsible for the piping through the village and for the erection of the fountain in its centre. Two stonemasons from Connemara carried out the work in cut stone on the fountain. The motto inscribed on the fountain is 'In the Desert a Fountain is Springing' and it cost £400 to construct.

The second half of the nineteenth century saw the establishment of tenants' associations throughout the country as the people agitated for ownership of land and improvements in their lives. Ballyvaughan and the neighbouring villages witnessed much activity. In September 1880 Charles Stuart Parnell made his famous speech in Ennis, County Clare, demanding that landlords who refused to give better living conditions to their tenants, including rent reductions, should be boycotted. Three months later a huge meeting was held in Ballyvaughan and people from all over North Clare, Gleninagh, Bell Harbour, Fanore, Corofin, Lisdoonvarna and Ennistymon came together. The village and all roads leading to it were decorated with streamers of welcome, 'Céad Míle Fáilte', 'God Bless Parnell and his Gallant Band', 'The Land for the People'. Michael Davitt, MP, one of the founders of the Land League, sent a letter of apology for his absence. Gorman Mahon, Home Rule MP for Clare, addressed the meeting. The parish priest, Fr Skerrit, also spoke and said, 'Last year while all the landlords were making concessions to their tenants, Colonel Whyte made no reductions, indeed had never set foot here, in union with Mr Lane Joynt, now fattening in Dublin.' This was the first recorded note of dissent against this landlord and his agent.

The landlord's agent, Lane Joynt, called a meeting at his residence, Clareville. A 25 per cent reduction on rent was offered and was refused by Miss Kate Hellatt (daughter of the late Church of Ireland rector), as she was demanding a 40 per cent reduction. A compromise was reached after the meeting.

In 1891, on the death of Parnell, the Ballyvaughan Board of Guardians tabled a motion, 'He was the only true and matchless leader of the people of all Ireland.'

During the First World War, a number of North Clare men joined the British services and later the American forces. Three local men lost their lives at the infamous Battle of the Somme,

View of the Burren coastline
© Karin Funke

others returned injured and many lived to ripe old ages in spite of their hardships and suffering.

After the rebellion in 1916, the villages of Fanore, Gleninagh, Ballyvaughan and Bell Harbour, and indeed the whole of County Clare, joined in the national struggle for independence. Numerous raids by the Black and Tans were carried out, especially on the homes of those suspected of involvement with the rebels, and many houses were ransacked and even burned down.

My mother, Kathleen Hyland, who was aged twelve at the time, told me that a small company of coastguards used to march to the village of Ballyvaughan each week for mail and supplies. A unit of Volunteers decided to attack them – mainly to capture their arms, but the coastguards resisted and at least two were killed. The local people were sorry because they knew the families, and the coastguards' children attended the local school, and they were extremely frightened because they feared reprisals, which came two days later. The noisy tenders of the Black and Tans could be heard approaching the village. My mother remembered that the priest lodged in our house and kept the petrol for his car in what was known as the summerhouse at the top of the orchard (now the car park of Hyland's Hotel). She raced to the summerhouse and found two full drums of petrol and many empty ones. She put the full ones in the middle of the stack, surrounding them on the top and sides with the empties. She heard the English accents of the Tans as they approached and she ran away. She climbed a tree, spied on the men, and saw one of the men lift some of the drums, but finding them empty, he threw them down, calling to his fellow soldiers that they were no good. They then went away. She always believed that she had saved the village from burning that day. A reign of terror lasted for several days, with the Tans trying to get information and the names of the Volunteers, but the local people didn't know them because the Volunteers were not local.

During the 1920s the fishing industry went into decline in Ballyvaughan but Gleninagh remained an important fishing village. Most of the catch was sold on Gleninagh Pier, was then transported to Ardrahan railway station and went by rail to the Dublin fish market. A few Gleninagh fishermen brought fish to the nearby villages each week. From about the 1880s until the 1930s the local Pouldoody oysters were among the most prized in fashionable London and Dublin society. Unfortunately, the oyster beds were wiped out by disease.

In 1932 the political party Fianna Fáil was elected to government, with Éamon de Valera as Taoiseach – he was known as 'Dev'. His government withheld the Land Annuities, the payments to the landlords, laid down in the various Land Acts and Land Purchase Acts of the nineteenth century. English landlords still owned much of the land of Ireland and retaliation was swift, resulting in an embargo by Britain on all Irish goods. This was the third war: the War of Independence, the Irish Civil War and then the Economic War which left the economy shattered. Our only industry was agriculture and our only market was closed, so farmers were forced to sell cattle solely for their hides – to make leather. The Irish government set up free food centres throughout the country, such was the need of the people. Rural villages like Ballyvaughan, Bell Harbour, Gleninagh and Fanore, in common with the rest of the countryside, did not escape. The weekly markets and fairs went into decline or ceased altogether and many business people as well as farmers had great difficulty surviving. However the majority of the population supported the refusal to pay the Land Annuities because it was believed that the land should belong to the people and not to foreign landlords. The Economic War lasted until the outbreak of the Second World War, when food supplies to England from the colonies – Australia, New Zealand, Canada – dwindled because of German naval activities, so the embargo on Irish produce was lifted.

Compulsory tillage was then introduced, which brought great activity; although the Burren land does not have deep topsoil it is very fertile in the valleys. Each farmer had a quota and was compelled to sow nearly every acre deemed suitable for the cultivation of crops, mainly sugar beet, grain and vegetables. The markets and fairs were revived. A spin-off was the harvesting of seaweed in the springtime, from March to early May, which was used as fertiliser for crops, and it was the only fertiliser available. Each day as many as a hundred men, known as meitheals, worked non-stop on the shore and the little off-shore islands until the tides forced them to stop. Then the seaweed was cut, collected into a rectangular pile, securely tied with ropes. This was called a climín and could float on the rising tide, and the men brought it in to the shores at Clareville and the Weathercock. From there, horses and creels (baskets) took it inland. All of this activity led to great comradeship and closeness in the entire area from Finavarra to Fanore, from coast to hills. Young men, given some land by their parents, were paid for working at the seaweed and for the crops. They used every little cove and pier, each one having its own workers. (However, in Ballyvaughan they never

Climín at Bell harbour harvesting the seaweed
© Irish Press

infringed one quay – Girls' Quay – which was the sole and private property of the ladies [between Clareville House and Burren House]. It had a good alcove of trees where the modest ladies could disrobe and go swimming.)

With the end of the Second World War compulsory tillage ceased and many jobs were lost. This, together with the closure of the phosphate mines operated by Judge Comyn in Doolin and Noughaval, led to mass unemployment and then to emigration – the pattern for the 1940s through the 1950s and into the 1960s. The weekly markets and fairs ceased and the roads no longer saw carts or vans.

Tourism was not taken seriously then. The occasional botanist came to the Burren in May, the special time for spring gentians, orchids and mountain avens. One excursion, in 1949, included a party of scientists from England who came to look for rare species of moth found only in the Burren. They stayed in what is now Hyland's Burren Hotel, then called Bray's Private Hotel, and the local people were attracted by the vehicles – huge vintage cars. The party worked at night on the surrounding hills with powerful generators, always hoping to see the moths. Crowds went to view these strange men in action and they were nicknamed 'fly-catchers'. During their week's stay, they found a number of rare specimens, among them the now famous Burren green moth.

The year 1952 saw the villages join the Rural Electrification Scheme. Before the arrival of electricity, a small number of people had installed wind chargers (now called wind turbines). I remember my grandfather installing one on his chimney. He spent a lot of his time making the wooden sails in his workshop, and because they had to survive the west of Ireland gales, they had to be replaced often. It charged quite a number

View of Ballyvaughan village
© Karin Funke

of batteries, providing light in the house and charging the radio batteries. This was greatly appreciated for listening to the hurling and football matches held on Sundays during the summer (men were not free to play on Saturdays because it was a working day – six-day week). On these days the sitting-room was packed, and when it was fine, crowds stood outside the windows to listen to Micheál O'Hehir's commentary.

History, as we know, deals with change. It is about people, their lives, livelihoods and their very survival, and here we attempt to show the changes wrought in the Burren coastal villages through the 1940s and afterwards, with a few flashbacks to earlier times. The past is remembered, the present made memorable by contrast and continuation, as we move from ruined castles and villages to discovery and development.

Ballyvaughan and the War of Independence 1919–1921

Justin Walsh

During the years 1919–1921 Ballyvaughan shared the experiences of upheaval and bloodshed of the War of Independence with the rest of the county – Clare had been under military rule since February 1918. The crown had lost the allegiance of the county and the people no longer recognised the administrative machinery of British rule. Sinn Féin controlled the county council, chaired by local man Peter O'Loghlen, and this council ignored Dublin Castle. Republican agents collected rates; Sinn Féin assumed policing duties and justice was decided by republican courts. IRA flying columns fought with the Royal Irish Constabulary (RIC) for control of the countryside and later engaged in guerrilla warfare with the Auxiliaries, the Black and Tans and British army.

The IRA unit active in the Ballyvaughan area was organised as H Company of the 5th Battalion of the Mid-Clare Brigade, under Captain Seán McNamara and Lieutenants Michael Mullins and Anthony O'Donohue. In February 1921, this became the core of the new 6th Battalion of the Mid-Clare

Brigade. In the beginning, its focus lay in ostracising the RIC from the community and, if the opportunity arose, seizing arms by raiding barracks or ambushing patrols. Before 1918, the RIC in North Clare were already in an embattled position. They had to police the deep-seated tensions over land, which often erupted into agrarian crime. However, they initially retained some support in the community. Some people were warned, with threats of violence, to end their business with the constabulary by no longer providing them with food or turf. Shots were fired into homes and warning notices posted. Despite this, some land owners, mindful of the RIC's role in the protection of their property, continued to support them and so required police protection. In January 1920, the IRA ambushed a party of police guarding a local farmer and the RIC replied with grenades, apparently the first time this weapon had been used by the police in County Clare, and scattered their assailants. Nevertheless, the IRA policy was successful and the RIC, too exposed in their small barracks across the Burren valleys, eventually became concentrated in Lisdoonvarna.

The rejection of the RIC had other consequences in the village. Sara J. Hoare, the principal teacher of the Girls' National School, was married to a local RIC sergeant who became a district inspector for North Clare. A Treasury memo considering her later application for compensation noted: 'His activities made him unpopular with a large section of the inhabitants of the district, and his wife shared in this unpopularity.' Her unpopularity rocketed following her husband's promotion and her position as a teacher in Ballyvaughan was threatened, as parents were encouraged to boycott the school. The IRA forcibly removed the key of the school from her and ordered her to leave Ballyvaughan on 21

February 1921. Following a week's closure of the school, the parish priest had persuaded students to return, but after two days the IRA reinstated their boycott and, because parents held to the boycott, the teachers sat in an empty building until April, when Mrs Hoare's health broke down. She was suffering from 'neurasthenia, general disability and insomnia'. The school was re-opened in May following Mrs Hoare's departure, with the assistant teacher taking over.

Crown authority was not only represented by the RIC in the village but also by a coastguard station on the shore outside the village; it was one of fourteen stations built during the nineteenth century on the Clare coast. The coastguard crew stationed there was responsible for patrolling 47 miles of coast between the flanking stations of Liscannor to its left and Renmore to its right. In 1920, six men were stationed there and some were accompanied by their families. Normally concerned with excise patrols and lifeboat duties, the coastguard stations had also played an important role during the recent First World War, maintaining a lookout for German U-boats. The coastguard stations were a reminder of Britain's rule and, like the RIC barracks, they became targets for raids for arms. When the war deepened, the IRA carried out the complete destruction of the stations, denying their shelter to British forces.

An IRA party raided the Ballyvaughan station for arms just before midnight on 13–14 February 1920. The IRA knew that the coastguard stations had been ordered by the Admiralty to resist any raids with force. Station officers were given extra arms to maintain armed sentry patrols and to prepare defensive positions. The local IRA intelligence officer assumed the station had arms, unloaded from a motorboat seen three weeks previously. An inspection by the coastguard captain, H.

C. Somerville from Queenstown, had taken place, but had little impact if its purpose was to instil martial vigour among the men. The Ballyvaughan coastguards were indeed armed with pistols but they were not keen to militarise their workplace and homes. The guns were hidden away so that when the IRA raided, although they were not to hand to use, they were not discovered and seized. Even the sentry on night watch had placed his weapon out of reach by hiding it in a stable bucket.

On the night of the raid, the IRA first cut the telegraph wires and then, under cover of darkness, infiltrated the station grounds. The night watchman, Hill, was walking around the station with his dog. It was a bad night; bands of Atlantic rain and mist lashed the limestone walls of the buildings. Hill's watch was nearing its end and Miller, the station's chief officer, was due to oversee the change with his replacement. As Hill rounded the stables' corner, he was confronted and surrounded by armed men; two guns were pointed at him and he was easily taken prisoner. Moments later the station's commanding officer left his quarters. He went out unarmed, his own pistol broken and dismantled in the back of a kitchen cupboard. He was caught walking across the yard. Meanwhile the relief watchman left his quarters to assume his sentry duty. He too had no gun and was easily captured crossing the yard. Another coastguard was captured emerging from an outside toilet. The fifth coastguard held the keys to some buildings which the raiders wanted to search. His captive comrades called him out and he too was taken into custody. The sixth man was left undisturbed in his cottage with his wife, blissfully unaware of the raid. The IRA had taken control of the station.

The raiding party, led by Ignatius O'Neill, Mid-Clare Brigade, with the local captain, Seán McNamara, searched the station but found no pistols. Instead, they commandeered two telescopes, one missing a lens, a barrel and butt of a .22 pellet rifle belonging to the young son of Miller, some drill and signal books and a pair of binoculars. An IRA account speaks warmly of the coastguard men, and although the raiders must have been disappointed by their poor haul, the operation seems to have been carried out with good humour. The account by Andrew O'Donohue, an officer of the Mid-Clare Brigade, speaks of the prisoners and captors enjoying 'a sing-song' together. Although this was understandably omitted from Miller's report of the raid to the Admiralty, he does emphasise the gentlemanly manner of the raiders, commenting that the leader 'showed every consideration for the women and children and that the raid was carried out very coolly and quietly'. The raiders left the station warning the coastguards not to follow them as they were leaving sentries. The local RIC, who had not yet been withdrawn from the village, were not informed of the raid until after dawn.

Miller's superiors did not appreciate the ease with which the IRA had taken control of the station. They queried his lack of preparedness. Hill explained that he had chosen not to carry his revolver because he was afraid the IRA would have seized it if the station was raided. After the raid there was no attempt to rush the IRA sentries posted outside the gates because the coastguards felt that the more numerous and better armed IRA had the tactical advantage. In the days following the raid, Miller chose to return his weapons to Galway on the coastguard trawler *John Chivers* and said he was concerned 'that they [IRA] would raid again and we should lose them, as the station cannot be held by six men under the best of circumstances being exposed to surprise attack on all sides'. J. May, the coastguard's divisional officer, dismissed the reluctance of Miller and his men to counter-attack the withdrawing IRA as cowardice and wrote, 'that the chief officer and his crew were afraid to venture out'. Reports of Miller's failure to meet the raiders with lead were passed up along the coastguards' hierarchy from Ireland to the Admiralty in Whitehall. Admiral Tupper, having read the file, ordered 'Mr Miller be sent elsewhere as quickly as possible; he is not the class of officer that is required in these parts.'

Miller was not the only coastguard officer to face the IRA. Most other stations were being raided and lives were being lost. Challenged by demands elsewhere across an overstretched empire – such as rebelling Iraqi tribes who were unwilling to exchange Ottoman suzerainty for British rule – the British War Office was under immense pressure to source the manpower required to support the RIC and contain the IRA. They turned to the Admiralty for help to defend the Irish coastguard stations, which after all were Admiralty property. Despite Admiral Beatty's initial reluctance, on 28 May 1920 the British cabinet gave 843 men of the 8th Marine Battalion to the army. They were to garrison and defend the coastguard stations. They sailed from Plymouth in June on the battleships *Valiant* and *Warsprite* for Ireland. Irish-born Royal Marines or Roman Catholics were not to be drafted for service with the battalion. As the IRA campaign was very effectively obstructing easy communication for crown forces across the countryside, stations selected for garrisoning were chosen for their ease of supply by water rather than by road. Other than two coastguards who remained, twenty-five Royal Marines and a new coastguard commanding officer, J. Worsell, replaced Miller and the coastguard families. A garrison was also placed in Liscannor coastguard station. Stations which were not garrisoned were evacuated throughout the summer of 1920. The IRA, to prevent their re-occupation by crown forces, immediately burned most of them.

Discipline became a problem as the marines were splintered into the relatively isolated garrisons. Drunkenness and fighting took place. Private Helmore murdered Corporal Yates, one of the platoon, shortly after the arrival of the marines in Ballyvaughan. Despite regular sweeps by crown forces through the North Clare countryside, especially in the spring of 1921, the marine platoon remained a lonely military pocket on the North Clare coast. The RIC eventually left Ballyvaughan; the roads across the area were systematically blocked by the IRA, making it very difficult for the administration's motor patrols. In May 1921 the divisional commander of Clare's RIC ruefully noted in his monthly report to Dublin Castle that the obstruction of roads was 'likely to ruin the tourist season this summer'. Ballyvaughan's marine garrison, however, was not concerned by the scarcity of holidaymakers in the Burren, as they had become the target of the new 6th Battalion of the IRA's Mid-Clare Brigade.

In May 1921, IRA GHQ in Dublin was becoming impatient for more attacks in North Clare and was calling on the Mid-Clare Brigade to increase the intensity of the assaults on crown forces to relieve pressure elsewhere in the country. The earlier ambushes of military and police convoys in North Clare had become tactically more difficult, as these convoys were now larger and were reinforced with armoured cars, thus outgunning the IRA. Furthermore, these patrols' movements were co-ordinated and they were able to offer quick support to each other if needed. However, as GHQ emissaries made their way from Dublin, the Mid-Clare Brigade, under Seán McNamara, had pre-empted their concerns and had struck at the Ballyvaughan marines. The intention was to ambush the marine party in the village, and as well as inflicting casualties, to capture as many weapons as possible.

The local 6th Battalion assembled with reinforcements drawn from the 5th Battalion at the National School above Corkscrew Hill. They waited outside the village for intelligence on the marines' movements. The plan pivoted on the irregular visits of the marines to the village to pick up provisions and mail. The IRA knew that the marines, before coming to the village, would ring the post office to check whether there was post waiting for them. A runner would then inform the IRA when the marines were expected in the village. The ambush party waited a day before they received word that the marines were expected the following morning, Saturday 21 May. McNamara's men then took up positions in the village around 6 a.m. and waited. Apparently, according to one account, they were preparing to abandon their ambush positions almost five hours later when word came that ten marines were marching in extended formation towards the village and all but two were armed. The IRA Volunteers waited until the lead elements of the marine party reached the centre of the village. They then opened fire. In the first IRA volley two marines fell and the others immediately took cover in doorways and returned fire. Those first British casualties were twenty-four-year-old Henry Chandler from Great Yarmouth, who had screamed, 'I am hit' as he slumped to the ground, and nineteen-year-old, J. R. Bolton from Kent. Chandler had been in the rear of the party and died within minutes from a massive gunshot wound to his chest. Bolton, towards the front and just behind the marine sergeant, was riddled with gunshot pellets and gunshot wounds to the head and to his left leg. He died instantly. Two other marines, J. D. Levin and J. T. Currell, were injured during the five minutes of shooting. The IRA, under covering fire, then took the weapons from the dead and injured marines and retreated. When one of the injured was approached by an IRA Volunteer, he is reported to have said, 'What good will it do you to kill me? Am I not bad enough as I am?'

'We do not want to kill you. We only want the rifle,' the Volunteer said.

The IRA then withdrew. Marine witnesses at the following military enquiry in Galway exaggerated the size of the IRA force, claiming that a hundred men had attacked them. Equally, the IRA's Limerick Brigade was claiming the following day that seven marines had been killed.

Seven weeks later, on 9 July, in the fading light of the summer evening the coastguard station itself was attacked. The IRA, sniping from 200–250 yards away, broke several windows and wounded a marine. Two days later, the Truce was agreed.

The War of Independence in Ballyvaughan was over. The marines sailed home on their warships, the RIC never returned, the coastguard station became an abandoned ruin and the tourists eventually returned in their motorcars and charabancs.

Grandfather

Cathleen Connole (née O'Loughlin)

My grandfather, Mortimer O'Loughlin, returned from Australia in 1901 and bought the old parochial house of Glenaragh and the surrounding land. The marquis of Buckingham built the church in 1795 before Catholic Emancipation (1829) and it was the church for the area until St John the Baptist church was built in Ballyvaughan at the end of the nineteenth century. The land near the church contained a ring fort, Dun Torpa, so the residence, enclosed in a beautiful walled garden, was called Glenfort House. One of the leaders of the 1848 Rebellion, John Blake Dillon, escaped when Fr Ryder, the parish priest, hid him in Glenfort House. He was disguised as a priest, brought to Galway and then went on to America.

A close relative, Mick O'Loughlin of the Old IRA, on the run after the 1916 Rising, was sheltered by Mortimer, and the RIC raided the house and found an empty bed but with the sheets still warm. Mortimer's wife stepped in and said she would report this harassment of 'innocent' people to her sister, Katie, wife of Tom Neylon, chief of the RIC in Sligo. The RIC were confounded and left.

On another occasion, Mick O'Loughlin narrowly escaped by lying hidden inside the wall across the road from Glenaragh House while the Tans, discussing what they would do with him when they caught him, discarded the butts of their cigarettes over the wall on top of him.

Ballyvaughan Castle –
a Lost Landmark

Paul Gosling

'Out of sight, out of mind' the old saying goes and it could
certainly be applied to Ballyvaughan Castle, one of the village's

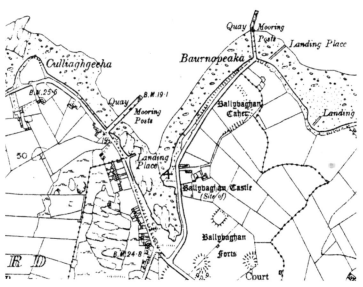

*Extract from the OS six-inch scale (1:10,560) map of 'Ballyvaghan' (Co.
Clare, Sheet 2), edition of 1915. The site of the castle is indicated by an
equal-armed cross just above and to the left of the B of 'Ballyvaghan Castle'*

more important yet now invisible monuments. My first serious engagement with the place occurred in 1993 when Keith Payne, artist, and the Ballyvaughan Development Group proposed a scheme to erect a stone sculpture entitled 'Mountains of Ireland: Stone Circle' on the site of the castle. It was to consist of a circular alignment of twenty freestanding stones, each one from a different mountain in Ireland. I was commissioned to pen an archaeological implications report on it but the scheme never went ahead and the castle site remains today, as it did then, a neglected and half-forgotten spot but one which is fundamental to any understanding of Ballyvaughan's history.

The site of Ballyvaughan Castle is located in the townland of Ballyvaughan, the Civil Parish of Drumcreehy, the Barony of Burren and the County of Clare. It is a recorded monument under the National Monuments Acts 1930–2004 and is included in the *Record of Monuments & Places* – RMP CL002-051.[1] Its Irish grid reference is 122942, 208158 and the site is not more than one metre above the high water mark.

The site is located on the east shore of a small, narrow inlet at the inner (southern) reaches of Ballyvaughan Bay (*see image p. 53*). This inlet is markedly tidal in character, being almost completely dry at low water. In wet weather, a small freshwater stream debouches into the southern end of the inlet but its bed is more frequently dry than wet. The OS maps show a number of other monuments in the immediate vicinity, including three ring-fort-like enclosures *c.*160-300m to the south-east. These are labelled on the maps as 'Ballyvaughan Forts'. There is also a much larger enclosure to the north-east of the castle site, labelled 'Ballyvaughan Caher' on the same map.[2] Though now partly

1   See www.archaeology.ie.
2   Described by Westropp 1901, pp. 278–9.

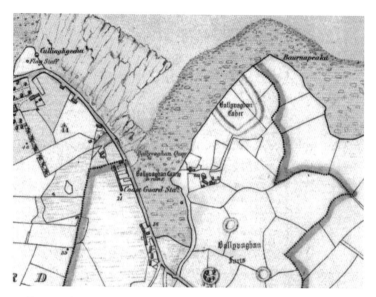

*Extract from the OS six-inch scale (1:10,560) map of 'Ballyvaghan'
(Co. Clare, Sheet 2), edition of 1842. 'Ballyvaghan Cas. (in ruins)' is
shown as a small square roofed building.*

effaced, its sub-rectangular plan and its size (NE-SW *c*.100m;
NW-SE *c*.80m) would lead most archaeological minds to mutter
'medieval' if squeezed for a date. Thus it could potentially be
contemporary with or a direct forerunner of the castle.

Today the castle site lies 400 metres north–north-west of
the centre of the modern village of Ballyvaughan. It is situated
on the western side of a relatively modern by-road which
runs northwards from the village to the pier and moorings at
Baurnapeaka. The pier at Baurnapeaka is known locally as the
'New Pier' to distinguish it from the 'Old Pier' on the opposite
(western) side of the inlet near Monks public house. According
to the late MacNeill O'Loghlen, an authority on local history,
the New Pier and the by-road leading to it were built 'about
1870 because it was nearer the channel'.

Though MacNeill could not be certain about the date of the old pier, its construction certainly post-dates the first edition of the OS six-inch map (*see image p. 55*), which was surveyed in 1840. On this map, an even older landing place is shown to the south-east of Monks on the western side of the inlet. This may be the 'quay' erected by the fishery board in 1829.[3] It appears on the first edition map as a semi-circular area *c.*30m across which is labelled 'Ballyvaghan Quay'. According to Mr O'Loghlen, this spot was used in his father's time for tarring the main masts of large hookers, but its area is much reduced by coastal erosion.

Very little is known regarding the architecture, date or history of the castle. We do not even know for certain what it looked like. No contemporary descriptions of it have survived and it does not appear to have attracted the eye of eighteenth- and early nineteenth-century landscape artists. However, at least three tiny cartographic representations of it are known. The earliest comes from the notebooks of the famous antiquarian Thomas Johnson Westropp. In them he presents a series of diminutive pen sketches of castles in County Clare which he evidently copied/traced from a now lost 'survey' made 'circa 1675'.[4] Now widely referred to as the 'Edenvale Castle Survey', it includes a sketch of 'Ballyvahane', which is numbered '97'. This sketch depicts the castle as a much ruined tower of three storeys, one corner/half of which has fallen (*see image p. 57*).

What events brought the castle to such a state of ruin at this early date are unknown, but it is recorded that the English authorities deliberately undermined the stairwell corners of many tower houses in the later seventeenth century to render

---

3   Cunningham 1980, p. 38.
4   Ó Dálaigh *et al.*, 2005.

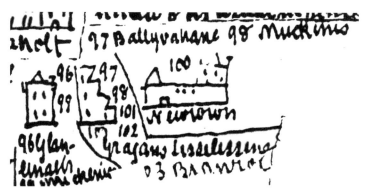

Extract from T. J. Westropp's notebooks (Royal Irish Academy, MS 3A 40, p. 224) showing tracings of Co. Clare castles from the so-called 'Edenvale Castle Survey' made c.1675. 'Ballyvahane' castle is labelled '97'. Four other numbers also appear beside the sketch. No. '98' refers to 'Muckinis' and '101, 102, 103' appear to refer to 'Gragans', 'Lissilissine' (Lissylisheen) and 'Branroe' (Binroe). For further details on these latter castles see Ó Dálaigh et al. (2005, 46-7).

them useless.[5] In fact, Ó Dálaigh's analysis of the 112 castles included in the 'Edenvale Castle Survey' shows that only 36 (32%) of them are depicted as roofed.[6] He attributes this to the Cromwellian wars and the decline of the castle *per se* as fashionable living quarters.

The second representation dates from 1776 where it appears on a maritime chart of Galway Bay.[7] Thereon it appears as an intact building of three storeys with a crenellated parapet (*see image p. 59*). Given the evidence of the 1675 representation this is at first puzzling until it is realised that Newtown Castle is also shown in exactly the same manner, albeit fractionally bigger! In fact the depiction of castles on Mackenzie's chart

---

5   Westropp 1899, p. 360.
6   Ó Dálaigh *et al.*, 2005, p. 39.
7   Mackenzie 1776, Chart XII.

is conventional rather than representing their actual state of repair. However, the presence of Ballyvaughan Castle on the chart indicates that significant portions of its fabric still stood in the late eighteenth century and that it was still a locally important landmark for mariners.

The third representation of the castle appears on the first edition of the OS map for County Clare (*see image p. 55*) which was surveyed in 1840. On it, the castle is shown as an almost square building, *c.*10m in maximum dimension. Though it is represented as a roofed structure (the interior is hatched) on this map, the contemporary Ordnance Survey Letters record that 'it is now destroyed and the site encroached upon by the sea. A few fragments of its walls, scattered about, are the only vestiges remaining.'[8] These vestiges appear to have been completely removed in the latter part of the nineteenth century so that not a stone of the castle itself remains visible today. According to Mr O'Loghlen its stone was used in the construction of the New Pier at Baurnapeaka which was built *c.*1870. Work on this pier included the construction of a new road which skirts the east side of the castle site and involved considerable raising of the ground surface immediately to the south-east of it. The stoutly built drystone walls which flank this road are also pointed out as having been constructed of stones taken from the castle.

H. G. Leask[9] once put the total number of castles in Ireland at 'over 2,900' but only one still retains its original wooden roof.[10] And when the roof went so did the furniture and with the furniture went the documents! Thus most Irish castles have

---

8   O'Flanagan 1928, Vol. 1, p. 28. Note: see also: http://www.clarelibrary. ie/eolas/coclare/history/osl/drumcreehy2-three-castles.htm.

9   Leask 1951, p. 153.

10   McNeill 1997, p. 217.

Extract from a maritime chart of Galway Bay published in 1776 (Mackenzie 1776). The castles at Ballyvaughan and Newtown (to left of tree) are clearly shown.

no surviving history and the occasional documentary fragments that survive are difficult to 'read', let alone knit into a narrative. Ballyvaughan Castle is a case in point. However, there is at least a little flurry of references to it in the English documentary sources of the later sixteenth century and Martin Breen and Risteárd Ua Cróinín[11] have gathered these together.[12]

The surviving references are concerned, for the most part, with matters of ownership and so provide little in the way of archaeological, let alone topographical, detail. However, there is the occasional insight such as the statement made by the anonymous author of the *Description of Ireland,* written in 1598, who wrote of 'Ballivaghan belonging to Sir Turloghe O'Bryen' alongside 'Bonrattie', 'Clare, 'Inchequin' and three other castles as the 'Principall Castles' of County Clare.[13]

---

11 Breen and Ua Cróinín 2008, p. 7.
12 See also Johnson 2005.
13 Hogan 1878, p. 126.

Comments like this certainly make one take notice. So who built this 'principall' castle? Here again there is no certainty. Being the leading hereditary sept of the Burren, the O'Loughlins are the obvious candidates. However, in the earliest specific mention of the castle, which dates to the late 1540s, it is clearly part of the possessions of Murrough O'Brien (died 1551), the first Earl of Thomond.[14] And we know from a rare surviving Irish property deed that Murrough got possession of the 'townland [of] Ballybeghan' from the O'Loughlins as retribution for the theft of a cow.[15] Westropp dates this event to 'about 1540' and if this is correct then it is striking that the deed makes no mention of any castle.[16] Did the O'Briens capitalise on their new possession by building the castle at Ballyvaughan in the 1540s or was the castle excluded from the fortified lands?

The next significant historical reference is in 1569. Under that year the *Annals of the Four Masters* record that the Lord Justice of Ireland, Sir Henry Sidney, made a 'great hosting' to Cork and later Limerick and Galway, during which 'Cluain-Dughain [Cloonoan, near Rockvale] and Baile-Ui-Bheachain [Ballyvaughan] in Thomond were taken by the Lord Justice.'[17] Why these particular Clare castles should have been targeted is unclear. The suggestion made by the Reverend P. White that this was part of 'the first formal attempt to introduce Protestantism into Clare' is too simplistic.[18] It is more likely to have been part of Sidney's policy of undermining the power base of the Earls of Thomond and promoting divisions among the lesser chiefs.[19]

---

14 Westropp 1899, p. 350.
15 Hardiman 1828, pp. 30–2, no. X.
16 Westropp 1900, p. 296; 1901, p. 279.
17 O'Donovan 1854, Vol. 5, p. 1633.
18 White 1893, p. 186.
19 Lennon 2005, p. 243.

In the years that follow, the castle continues to appear sporadically in the English documentary sources. While these references are invariably brief, they do serve to illustrate the perilous nature of land (and castle) ownership in Ireland at the time. In 1570 for instance, the castle is recorded in the state papers of Elizabeth I as being 'with the barron [*sic*] of Inchiquin', possibly a direct consequence of its seizure by Sidney the previous year.[20] However, by 1574 another state paper lists it along with every other castle in the Barony of Burren as being in the possession of 'OLoghlen'.[21] The O'Loughlins were undoubtedly the leading hereditary sept in the Burren and their possession of the castle is confirmed by another reference dating to 1580 which mentions it and three other castles in the Parish of Drumcreehy as being 'by an O'Loghlen'.[22] However, by 1584 it appears once again as part of the possessions of one of the O'Brien's, as an inquisition at Ennis in January, 1585 found that Turlogh O'Brien of Smithstown (died 1584) was the owner of a number of estates in the county including 'Ballyvaghan castle and lands'.[23] Turlogh was still in possession of it in 1598 (see above) and thereafter, wherever it pops up in documents, its ownership is solidly with the O'Briens.[24] The latest of these references is dated 1646, when a deed leasing various parcels of land in Clare to one Christopher O'Brien 'of Inistyman' for three years, includes 'the half quarter and the three parts of a castle in Ballyveaghane'. This is just after the Rebellion of 1641 but before the Cromwellian campaigns of

---

20 Breen 1995, p. 134.
21 Twigge 1909, p. 82.
22 Frost 1893, pp. 24–5.
23 *Ibid.*, p. 270.
24 See Westropp 1899, p. 352; Frost 1893, p. 439; Ainsworth 1961, pp. 348–9, no. 1069.

the early 1650s; however, it is not known what state the castle was in at this time.

A relatively small D-shaped grassy area measuring approximately 34.6m north–south and 46.5m east–west now marks the site of Ballyvaughan Castle. This is defined along the straight eastern side by the road from the village to the New Pier and on the other sides by the tidal inlet (*see image below*). Access is via a modern field gate centrally placed in the roadside boundary wall. The grassy area is almost level but is very bumpy and stony underfoot. It is currently (April 2009) being grazed by horses.

When I first visited in December 1993, the curving edge

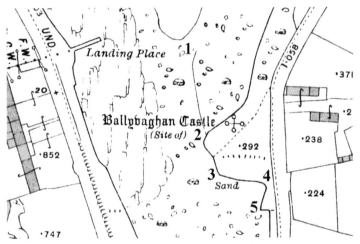

Extract from the OS twenty-five-inch scale (1:2,500) map of 'Ballyvaghan' (Co. Clare, Sheet 2, XV), edition of 1915. The site of 'Ballyvaghan Castle' is shown by a cross, just outside the north-west limits (indicated by a broken line) of the triangular grassy area (indicated by '.292' acres). The line 1-2 is probably the last vestige of the western wall of the castle's bawn. The map also shows the position of its southern continuation at 3. This joins up with an old quay wall (4-5), which appears to have protruded from the south end of the bawn but is now partly overlain by the modern roadway.

of the grassy area from west to south-west was delimited by a low scarp face up to one metre in height, but very little of this is now visible. In 1993 the exposed section faces revealed soil profiles dominated by a compact yellow boulder clay, but these deposits appeared to be almost entirely modern.[25] When coupled with information from Mr O'Loghlen, this suggested that much of the south-west part off the grassy area is composed of modern fill.

A comparison between the present limits of grassy area and those shown on the 1915 and 1842 editions of the OS six-inch scale maps indicates that it has not changed greatly since the early nineteenth century. However, on the twenty-five-inch version of the 1915 map (*see image p. 62*) it is clear that the site of the castle is actually indicated just outside the northern limits of the grassy area on the stony foreshore. This suggests that considerable erosion has occurred since medieval times. This map also shows a wall running roughly north–south from the edge of the grassy area out into the inlet itself (*p. 62, points 1–2*). The line of this wall can still be traced on the ground as a ruinous seaweed-covered drystone revetment running north-south for a distance of *c.*39m. It is built of large boulders neatly placed and is up to 2.4m in height. It appears to be turning slightly eastwards at its north end but it terminates raggedly shortly thereafter. Breen and Ua Cróinín label this feature as 'an old pier wall' but it is clearly more of a revetment than a freestanding pier.[26] Furthermore, its line can also be traced southwards from point 2 for a further 34m as an intermittent line of large limestone blocks just protruding from the shingle foreshore along the west-south edge of the grassy area (*p.*

25 See Gosling 1993.
26 Breen and Ua Cróinín 2008, p. 7.

View looking northwards, showing the tops of the limestone boulder revetment as exposed in the shingle foreshore along the west side of the grassy area (p. 62, no. 3). The tape is 3m long. The northward continuation of the revetment (p. 62, nos 1–2) is just visible in the top background as a black, seaweed-covered area
© P. Gosling

62, points 2–3). At point 3, it appears to turn/curve sharply eastwards and runs in a straight line to join up in a boldly executed curve with an old quay wall (*p. 62, points 4–5*) at the south-west limits of the site. This quay wall is also constructed of large, roughly squared boulders up to five courses and 2.1m in height. It is 13.5m in length and at least 10.6m in width – it is partially overlain by the road to the New Pier (*see image p. 65*). Though now in ruins, it was obviously finely built originally.

Though it is not possible to be definitive about the date of these walls and revetments, their character and configuration suggest that they are the last vestiges of the bawn wall of the castle. If so, the bawn measured at least 73m north–south by 38m east–west. It also appears to confirm the statement in the OS Letters that the site of the castle was 'encroached upon by the sea'.[27] If this is the

---

27   O'Flanagan 1928, Vol. 1, p. 28.

View looking south-west, of the finely built drystone quay at the southern extremity of the grassy area (Ill. 5, nos 4-5). Note the finely wrought curve in the masonry at its northern end (on left) where it joins the southern revetment of the bawn. The modern wall in the background is the sea-wall of the Baurnapeaka road
© P. Gosling

case then much of the northern part of the bawn interior as well as the castle may well have been destroyed by erosion. However, only archaeological excavation could (dis)prove this point.

Fragmentary as the foregoing is, I will now attempt a speculative narrative on the castle's history. This will demand bold (and possibly inaccurate) guesswork since so much is lost or imprecise, but if it provokes disagreement then it will have succeeded.

So, sometime in the 1540s Murrough O'Brien, the first Earl of Thomond, built a stone castle on an inlet of Ballyvaughan Bay. He had only recently gained possession of this valuable haven through a fine placed on the local Ó Lochlainn or O'Loghlen sept. The new multi-storeyed crenellated tower dominated the navigable approaches to Baile Uí Bheachain as well as the old earthen Ó Lochlainn bawn to the north-east. The new castle was much more prestigious and its stone-walled bawn was particularly impressive, rising straight out of the tidal waters. At its south end, it incorporated a short stone wharf where boats could berth at full tide, loading and offloading directly on to the quayside. In fact, it was the opportunities which sea-trade could bring which likely influenced the O'Brien to build here for Baile Uí Bheachain or Ballyvaughan had potential as a trading spot on a coastline with few comparable safe havens. The castle was also strategically important as a symbol of O'Brien power in the northern part of the Burren, traditionally the stronghold of the Ó Lochlainns. Then came 1569 and the treacherous land and sea attack by the forces of the Lord Justice Sidney. He gave possession of the castle to the Earls of Inchiquin, but the Ó Lochlainns quickly got control of the castle and held this valuable prize for over a decade. By the mid 1580s, however, the Earls of Thomond had regained it and by the close of the 1500s it was regarded as one of the principal castles of the new County of Clare, ranked alongside Bunratty and Inchiquin. While it was held peaceably for the first third of the new century it, like many other Clare castles, fell foul of the political and military upheavals in the wake of the rebellion of 1641. By the 1670s it was in a ruinous state, having been wilfully slighted with gunpowder by civilian contractors acting on behalf of the Cromwellian administration in Ireland. The O'Briens and Ó Lochlainns were by now much reduced in circumstances. The tower was riven from top to bottom and the walls of the bawn may well have been partially breached at the seaward end. As the following years became decades the sea took back in stone what it had given in wealth so that by the time the measuring men of the ordnance department came in the 1830s there was nothing left but 'a few fragments … scattered about'.

Thanks to Keith Payne, who first aroused my interest in the castle; to Mr MacNeill O'Loghlen (RIP) for information on local history; to Anne Korffe for first drawing my attention to the 'Edenvale Castle Survey'; and to the staffs of the Special Collections Room, Hardiman Library, NUI Galway, and the Local Studies Centre, Clare County Library, Ennis.

Newtown Castle, Ballyvaughan, before 1914
© *Lawrence Collection, Courtesy of the National Library of Ireland*

Second World War

Mortimer O'Loughlin

There was of course a shortage of food and fuel and other supplies in Clare during the Second Word War and rationing was introduced, with ration cards distributed. Farmers grew extra crops to cope with the situation.

There was no running water in those times. Women drew buckets of water from the fountain in the centre of Ballyvaughan as well as from a spring in Hyland's field opposite the church and at Lisanard, Ballyconry and the Pinnacle Well, Ballyvaughan. People also drew water from a spring called 'Caher Gheal'. There were also troughs for animals at Muckinish

The coastline of the Burren
© Karin Funke

and Newtown. Blankets were washed in the Rathborney River, where it re-emerged near Ballyvaughan, and were laid out to dry on the limestone rocks.

There was no coal but there was the life-saving turf. The bog was up the Corkscrew Hill and was owned by Frank Martyn of Gregan Castle. An annual rent was paid for the right to cut turf. This right was not available to all, so hazel, blackthorn, whitethorn and ash were also burned.

The majority of births took place at home, assisted by the local midwife, Nurse Tynan, and the local doctor, Dr Batty Quinn. Husbands were not present at the birth, unlike today, but the neighbouring women also helped. It was said that Nurse Tynan always carried a bottle of whiskey with her.

Tuberculosis was rampant during the 1940s and deaths from this disease were many. Gleninagh was especially affected – it was believed locally that this was because of the lack of light with the sun being cut off by Gleninagh Mountain.

In spite of the hard times, there were dances in the houses but these were frowned on by the church and later by the state – the gardaí were liable to visit the house where the dance was held. Later the house dances ceased and dances were held in a local hall – easier to supervise perhaps!

The little church near Lough Rask, Ballyvaughan, was, in a much appreciated gesture by the representative body of the Church of Ireland, sold to the Roman Catholic bishop of the diocese. It was dismantled stone by stone, each one being marked and re-erected at Noughaval, near Kilfenora. Transport was by horse and cart up the Corkscrew Hill. It was dedicated in 1943 and named St Mochua's church.

There were many displaced men and women walking the roads during the war, old soldiers from the First World War, poets, dismissed teachers, former inmates of workhouses (all were closed), silenced priests (priests who were forbidden to say mass in public, hear confessions or administer to the people, usually for some offence like indiscipline or being too fond of the drink). Many of the displaced came to the villages and were given shelter in the kitchen – they slept before the open fires.

The 1940s marked the end of a century or more of darkness for the coastal villages of the Burren, indeed for the whole Burren. Gradually there were improvements, changes which eased the daily lives of its people: running water, electricity, farm machinery, transport, etc. The little asses disappeared to be replaced by Model-Ts and other makes of car. The old skills declined: roof-thatching, basket-making, scything, the old way of seaweed-gathering, etc.

The Second World War and the Burren
Brendan O'Donohue

It was no exaggeration to say that people in Ireland and of course in the coastal villages feared an invasion during the Second World War, the only doubt being which of the protagonists would come, the English or the Germans. The government initiated local defence forces, the LDF and LSF, to defend and patrol the coasts and rivers. The Black Head coastguard station was built in 1939–1940 by the Department of Defence to monitor unusual sea activities and report them to the local gardaí. Three permanent staff were employed in eight-hour shifts, John Scanlon, Seán Conway and John Linnane (captain).

Local people living near Gleninagh Castle held that German submarines regularly refilled with water from the well near the castle. Lights were seen, music was even heard and

*Fanore church and the Caher river in Caher valley (known
locally as the Khyber Pass)*
© *Karin Funke*

both were reported to the gardaí but not to the media. One
night when John Scanlon was cycling to work at Black Head,
he was thrown from his bicycle over the sea wall. He was found
by the gardaí and was off work for three weeks. It was said that
foreign soldiers had beaten him. However the truth was that
a donkey had been asleep in the middle of the road and both
it and John frightened each other so much that the accident
occurred.

News of the war was in great demand so the *Irish Press*
newspaper was invaluable. It didn't always arrive but when it
did it was passed from person to person. Radio Éireann only
broadcast from 9 p.m. to 10 p.m. However, a returned Irish-
American in Doolin rigged up a huge contraption, a pole
made from ass cartwheels and shafts complete with aerial
and antenna, which could pick up BBC news. Jamsie Woods,
known as Jamsie Caoilte, was a regular listener and went about

O'Donohue's Pub, Fanore
© *Karin Funke*

recounting all the news. People were delighted and put great trust in Jamsie's news flashes. One evening Jamsie heard on the news, 'The Japanese have invaded Bell Harbour', and ran out to tell everyone and especially the LDF. The defence forces rushed into their uniforms and lined up. One man, on hearing the news, shouted out, 'God, we've never been invaded by them before'. They were just about to march off to reinforce poor Bell Harbour when it was announced that it wasn't Bell Harbour at all but Pearl Harbour – way over in the Pacific Ocean. There was not the same trust in Jamsie after that.

Paddy Connolly tells of a day at the Ballyvaughan Fair during the war when word was spread that the village was crammed with soldiers and that there had been an invasion from Northern Ireland. Paddy's uncle, a member of the LDF, was alerted, 'Get up quick, we've been invaded again'. His uncle kissed his wife and family 'goodbye', all convinced they'd never see each other again. He was back within the hour – the soldiers were the Irish army on manoeuvres.

GAA in the Villages

Gerard Mahon

The man who is credited with developing and organising the distinctive games of hurling and football, Michael Cusack (1847–1907), was a native of our neighbouring parish of Carron. He published articles in nationalist newspapers in 1884 to appeal to the people to reject English sports and culture, which were widespread in Ireland at the time. (Athletes could compete only under the rules of the English Athletic Association.) He thought Irish people were abandoning their sports and activities that had been played in the open in fields and at crossroads for centuries. He thought they were demoralised by the Famine (1846–1852), poverty and English laws and that they had gone 'back to their cabins'. Cusack urged them to come out and play distinctively Irish games. He felt it would improve their physical condition and morale, discourage Anglicisation, give people an interest in Irish culture and traditions, and stimulate pride in place and nation.

Maurice Davin, a successful, well-known and respected international athlete and world record holder, wrote to the newspapers in support of Cusack's ideas and offered to help establish and run a sporting organisation. They held a meeting in Thurles on 1 November 1884 and those present, about thirteen people, founded the Gaelic Athletic Association, the GAA. They were supported by church leaders like Dr Croke, archbishop of Cashel, political leader, Charles Stewart Parnell, and Michael Davitt, the leader of the Land League, which was working for the redistribution of land. At a subsequent meeting, it was decided to form a club in every parish in the country.

Today we see a vibrant amateur organisation which at national level has one of the finest stadiums in the world. At local level, Ballyvaughan GAA club qualified in 2007 to play senior football for the first time since grading was introduced about eighty years ago.

When the founding fathers of the GAA established the organisation, it was as if they had tapped into a spring, releasing a surge of pride, passion, hope and enthusiasm which to this day elevates the spirit and nourishes those who follow in the footsteps of the founders. It provides inspiration for those who wish to promote through voluntary action, service and commitment what is best in our culture and tradition including sport, music and dance. The GAA has always been more than a sporting organisation. It has been a national movement.

As we have celebrated the 125th anniversary of its foundation, it is appropriate to reflect on the long journey undertaken in Ballyvaughan, Fanore and the small villages of the Burren region. In an area which shared the same countryside as Michael Cusack, it is fair to say that it has taken a long time to establish a successful club with its own playing field and the necessary facilities, and there were times when there was no team in the area. It took some years to have a proper organisation in place at county and parish levels.

Initially games were played between local parishes, which initiated rivalries that persist to this day. Ballyvaughan's first recorded participation in the Clare football championship was in 1907.

As far as can be established, Ballyvaughan and its region participated in championship games over a twenty-year period, up to the mid or late 1920s. A number of players for the club played for the county team.

Present-day tactics and organisation would have been frowned upon. Catch and kick was the method and the fielding of a ball high in the air was greatly admired. The direct route to goal was the preferred option. A high ball into the small square in front of the goal combined with a liberal interpretation of the rules was thought to yield the best results. This allowed the incoming forwards ample time to advance on the goalkeeper and to proceed to bury him in the net, if there was one, or in its absence to immobilise him against the fence at the back of the goal. It was a bonus if the goalkeeper ever had possession of the ball. If we could recapture images of this period, one outstanding feature would be that many players wore caps and even hats. Apparently many felt underdressed without their headgear and it was never removed except during the 'free for all' which followed some misdemeanour.

The organisation and development of the GAA games was greatly hampered from 1929 to 1960, the period which saw the Great Depression, the Economic War waged by England against Ireland and post-Second World War emigration. While the club did win a county title in the newly introduced intermediate grade in 1937, many players were forced to play in amalgamations with other clubs. However, there was always a hard core of players in the parish and young children often saw talented footballers displaying their skills in the workhouse field on fine Sundays, which helped to pass on the tradition to the next generation.

The tradition was also maintained and popularised by the coming of radio and the wonderful commentaries on the football and hurling games by Micheál O'Hehir (a Clareman). No one conveyed the sense and feel of the games like him, the thrill, the courage, the pride of contest and the superb speed. Single-handedly he was responsible for raising the profile of the games and the GAA. Inter-county GAA players became household names: some, such as Mick Mackey, Christy Ring, the Rackard brothers and Mick O'Connell, achieved legendary status. These players, as well as committed club members, mentors and trainers, inspired generations of players and supporters in sufficient numbers to maintain Gaelic games as Ireland's premier sports despite retaining their amateur status and having to compete with professional sports where billions are spent in promotion.

Transport to games presented a challenge up to the 1970s: on one occasion almost an entire underage team had to travel in the back of a van up Corkscrew Hill, which was 'stomach-churning'. Bad travellers were a curse, requiring frequent stops.

A GAA club without its own field is like a family without a home. A whole century had passed since the foundation of the GAA during which the Ballyvaughan area club was still dependent on the generations of various landowners who allowed their fields to be used for football practice. Numerous attempts had been made to acquire what was known as the 'workhouse field', but without success. A final effort was made in the 1980s and on this occasion the field was made available for community use. A large amount of levelling and in-filling was required when drainage problems arose, and the minimum dimensions for a football pitch necessitated in-filling right up to the animal pound wall. Clare County Council moved the pound and gave permission for the in-filling to begin. The field was widened a little and the new clubhouse was finished, in a manner in keeping with its stunning environment in the Burren.

The club now bears the name Ballyvaughan/Fanore GAA Club and is for all the people of the surrounding villages including Bell Harbour and Gleninagh. In 2007 the club won the county intermediate title, which gained the club senior status, by beating our near neighbours and foes, the Michael Cusack's club, who were hot favourites to win the title on the day. This brought unbounded joy and excitement to the whole area. Our club also beat the Ennis team, Eire Óg, who were recent county champions and one of the most successful teams in the competition, thus capping the club's achievements during its first year in senior grade.

To maintain a team at senior level is a huge task in a sparsely populated area because our team panel has just over twenty players. The present status of the club owes much to the voluntary efforts of a few dedicated people who put life and energy into coaching schoolchildren and the Under-12 age group, achieving success at county level with this team, and continuing with all the age groups up to Under-21 level. The teams show wonderful commitment and love of the sport and are worthy to continue the GAA tradition.

A positive development in modern times is the increased involvement and participation of women in what was a male-dominated organisation. While camogie was always popular, ladies Gaelic Football has become increasingly popular and is now played throughout the country.

By examining the establishment, evolution and continuation of the GAA, its integral place in Ireland today and over the past 125 years, there is every reason to conclude that it will adapt to and cope with all the challenges ahead. The GAA was founded during a time of great need for pride, self-reliance and self-respect. Just as the GAA helped our people in the past so it has its role today in helping our people to achieve a fair, just and inclusive society.

Discovery and Development
1940–2009

Nuala Mulqueeney

The Burren, a bare limestone plateau which extends over an area of more than 300 square kilometres, is home to Aillwee Mountain. It occupies a central location and is typical of the Burren uplands. At the foot of this mountain, just south of Ballyvaughan, a great character by the name of Jacko McGann was born in 1896.

As a child, Jacko played in the fields close to Aillwee but it seems that his first trip to the mountain itself, at the age of seven, was an adventure. He followed the family's herd of goats up the mountain. The day moved on and Jacko fell asleep only to wake up and find that night had fallen. Luckily, the alarm had been raised and a search party soon caught up with the young adventurer. As Jacko grew up his interest in Aillwee never diminished. In fact, it became more intense and when a farmer in the valley required a herdsman Jacko got the job and was delighted because it meant he could spend most of the winter months on the mountain.

It was during his tenure as a herdsman on the mountain that Jacko's venturesome spirit came to the fore once more, or perhaps on this occasion it was the wandering of his sheepdog that resulted in his seeing an entrance to an underground passageway. Jacko later recalled how his dog 'took off after a rabbit down a hole in the ground'. This passageway led to caverns and cascades that made up the cave system of Aillwee. Jacko made this discovery in 1944 and it was not the only underground discovery he made over the years. At this time the Burren had also become a destination for cavers exploring the numerous other cave systems that exist in this limestone region.

In the early 1970s Jacko shared his knowledge of the caves with a visiting group of potholers from the University of Bristol. Under the leadership of Dr Tratman, the cave system was formally explored and mapped, and it was noted that Aillwee Cave was relatively easily traversed because it was an exceptionally dry system of passageways and caverns.

Roger Johnson and Micheál Mulqueeney met at a Muintir na Tíre meeting in Kilfenora parish hall in 1973. Around that time a local cooperative had been set up in the North Clare area of Kilfenora, Carron and New Quay to develop a centre where both local people and visitors could come to learn about the Burren region, its geology, history and culture. It was believed that the centre could create and house a knowledge resource about this unique region while also providing employment and attracting visitors to the area.

Roger Johnson, his wife, Susan, and their three young sons, Nicky, Ben and Adam, arrived in Kilfenora in the late 1960s via Nottingham, England, Johannesburg, South Africa, and Dunloughlan, Connemara. Born in 1935, Roger grew up in Nottingham and studied to be a mining engineer. The family settled in Kilfenora and Roger bought an interest in a local quarry. Susan opened a craft shop called the Burren Bazaar.

Micheál Mulqueeney, born in 1938, was raised in Kilfenora. He worked in Germany, where he met his wife, Ani Auer. They settled back in Kilfenora and had a family of three, Josephine, Mark and Nuala. He taught German and geography at the Christian Brothers school in the nearby town of Ennistymon.

Roger and Micheál agreed that the Burren region had huge potential to attract visitors. Micheál, having grown up in the region, was very familiar with its unique landscape and the depth of historical importance the area offered. Roger, with his mining and engineering expertise, was looking for an enterprise on which to build a business. Both wanted to offer the visitor a truly original experience. Local knowledge and a keen interest in caving led the pair to a meeting with the head of the Geology Department at Trinity College Dublin, Dr David Drew.

Dr Drew knew the cave systems of the Burren region very well and brought them to Aillwee Mountain. He believed that Aillwee Cave had the greatest potential to be developed as a show cave. Because of its height above sea level it did not easily flood, so with some work it would be possible for people other than caving specialists to see the Burren from a completely different perspective.

Roger and Micheál purchased about 26 acres surrounding the cave, and development work began in 1974. The obvious name was taken from the mountain, Aillwee.

During excavation and initial development, many animal remains were found: examination of these identified them as horse and badger bones and, more interestingly, those of the European brown bear. Coupled with these was the discovery of hibernation pits – hollows scraped out in the ground to serve as resting places for the bears, so the trademark 'Brown Bear' for the Aillwee Cave was chosen. More development included electric lighting, flag-flooring and hand-railing of walkways. At this time, tourism in the area was in its infancy and the first group of visitors went through the cave in the summer of 1976.

Micheál and Roger, Ani and Susan along with a small staff, greeted visitors to Aillwee Cave and enabled them to explore the Burren's underground safely and comfortably. Over the next year or two, Aillwee Cave became better known and visitor numbers grew. All the while exploration of the cave was going on and a previously uncharted kilometre and a half of passageway was discovered after a boulder choke was penetrated.

With the growth in visitor numbers came the need for larger facilities. Even though Ireland had increasing unemployment and consequent emigration, as well as the troubles in Northern Ireland, it was decided to go ahead with plans for a new visitor facility. The resulting building, designed by Polish architects Andrzej and Danuta Wejchert, won several awards in the late 1970s and early 1980s.

The 1980s brought even more growth at Aillwee Cave. The tour route was lengthened to just short of a kilometre round trip. The cave was proving to be a popular day trip for school and university students, especially since the Burren region was being studied at both levels. As an employer in the area, Aillwee Cave went from strength to strength. At any one time in the year an eclectic group of very interesting people could be found working in the cave, their ages ranging from about sixteen to seventy. More development proceeded over the next two decades and one of the highlights was the production of Burren Gold – a distinctive farmhouse cheese made from cow's milk provided by one of the local dairy farmers. The cheese was, and is, produced in the cheese factory at the foot of Aillwee Mountain from March to October. This hard Gouda-style cheese with a variety of subtle flavours has won numerous culinary medals over the years.

Famous countrywide, Aillwee Cave also hosted events and became a great place to meet. An episode of *Father Ted* was filmed there, mime artist Marcel Marceau performed there and the fashionistas of the mid-west region showed off their designs at a clothing and fashion extravaganza at the site. Even Santa Claus decided that Aillwee Cave would be a fitting place to meet with children in his annual trek across the globe.

As Aillwee Cave came of age, its twenty-first birthday in 1997 was celebrated in style. In the twenty-one years since it opened to the public, over 700 people had worked there and were invited back not just to attend a party but to swap stories and experiences of their time at the cave.

As the well-documented Celtic Tiger roared from the 1990s into the new millennium, changes also came to Aillwee Cave. The evolution of the mini-break, thanks to low-cost travel, meant that the cave became more frequently visited in the months of January and February. As it became accessible year-round, full-time jobs became a reality, with a childcare facility for employees. Immigration also played a part – a rudimentary survey found that people from eleven countries were working at the cave and living in the vicinity.

The latest addition to the cave is the Burren Bird of Prey Centre. Since 2007 visitors have had an opportunity to come very close to hawks, owls, eagles and falcons. They are flown daily so that visitors can see their magnificence and splendour.

As Aillwee Cave grew, the desire to make visitors feel relaxed and comfortable while exploring the underground passageways was passed on to the next generation. Now the grandchildren of the Johnsons and Mulqueeneys help out during the school holidays. At Aillwee Cave memories are made and exciting experiences are shared.

The Burren College of Art – from Dream to Reality

Mary Hawkes Greene

In 1986, Michael Greene and his wife, Mary Hawkes, acquired Newtown Castle House, 22 acres and the ruined castle from Maura Collins. Preliminary work on the house revealed extensive structural problems that necessitated reducing the house to a bare shell. Roof, floors, windows and doors were all replaced. Newtown Castle House was reinvented as a guesthouse and opened in 1988. Within two years, the house was listed in 'the top hundred places to stay in Ireland' and was receiving widespread acclaim.

Mary and Michael originally thought they could restore the unique tower house, crumbling fast under the entangling ivy. However, the tower was connected to the Bardic and Brehon Schools of the sixth to sixteenth centuries, and to the monastic settlement of Corcomroe, an era when education flourished as scholars and creative people were drawn to the area by the special quality of the Burren. Inspired by this rich history and a desire to lessen the dependence of Ballyvaughan and its neighbouring villages on seasonal tourism, Michael decided to establish an art college. His vision was clear and simple: 'To create the greatest little art college in the world'.

*Restored
Newtown Castle,
Ballyvaughan
© Karin Funke*

A feasibility study revealed an opportunity to provide art education for students from the United States wishing to study in Ireland. An advisory council of luminaries from the arts assembled in Newtown with Mary and Michael over heady weekends of brainstorming, idea-bashing, tea-drinking and singing, and the concept of the Burren College of Art was finalised.

Crucial to these discussions was Professor Eugene Wicks, dean of the School of Art and Design at the University of Illinois at Urbana-Champaign. Gene was initially invited to develop programmes for the Burren College of Art which would meet the standards of United States' accrediting bodies. Captivated by the excitement of beginning a new idealistic art school and lured by the mysterious attraction of the Burren, Gene was appointed inaugural dean of the college in 1993. 'Tigín', a beautiful seafront cottage, became home to Gene and his wife Bonny for the following six years as they immersed themselves in every aspect of community life.

The college building was complete by January 1994, with assistance from Shannon Development. The tower continued to crumble and had to be refurbished before the college could open. Sixteen weeks later, the new roof was raised and the tower was restored to its former glory. President Mary Robinson officially opened the Burren College of Art and Newtown Castle Tower in July 1994. A new era had begun for the O'Loghlen stronghold and was appropriately celebrated at the first O'Loghlen clan gathering at Newtown Castle in 1995.

Since then, the college has been home to over 2,500 students, mostly from North America. The students live year-round in Ballyvaughan, contributing economically and culturally to the area. The college and castle are an integral part of the local community, hosting concerts, storytelling sessions, the annual Burren Spring Conference and Burren Law School. President Mary McAleese celebrated its achievement at the tenth anniversary celebration on 15 July 2004. Sadly, Michael was not there to witness it, having died as he was playing football for Ballyvaughan on the same date two years earlier.

The college, a not-for-profit charitable trust, now offers an international Master of Fine Arts (MFA) degree accredited by the National University of Ireland, Galway, in association with the Royal College of Art, London, and the School of the Art

Institute of Chicago. On a beautifully sunny 18 April 2005, the mace-bearer of the National University of Ireland led the robed academic procession from the steps of Newtown Castle around the college courtyard to confer the first ever master's degrees in a third-level college in County Clare. The ghosts of the O'Loghlens and the spirit of Michael Greene combined to smile on the occasion.

The college also hosts international students on semester and summer undergraduate programmes. During the summer months, week-long workshops open the college facilities to hobbyists pursuing courses ranging from botanical painting to digital photography. A new gallery and state-of-the-art studios opened in May 2005. It hosts an ongoing series of exhibitions, bringing the best of contemporary art to North Clare.

The college facilities and programme are now world renowned. Only one element remains to complete Michael's vision of creating 'the greatest little art college in the world' and that is making this experience available to the most talented students worldwide irrespective of means. The goal is to have all of the places fully funded through scholarships by 2015.

Mass Path Hike

Gordon D'Arcy

Ten years teaching Irish Studies at the Burren College of Art has revealed the Burren to me in a refreshingly new and most unexpected way. My usual mode of learning, by rambling on my own, continues to expose new findings, new perspectives; the Burren with its complex, multi-layered character lends itself to that sort of investigation. But seeing the place through the youthful eyes of overseas students – complete strangers to this old-world, rural setting – is another thing entirely.

Our Friday afternoon field trips have taken us from flooded turlough to grassy plateau, from cave maw to coast, from prehistoric megalith to Martello tower, from ancient cooking place to ring-fort cashels, all in the pursuit of the Burren story – and by extension, that of Ireland. The students, from all parts of the United States, having never been exposed to such rich and accessible heritage, are invariably bowled over by the experience. Learning 'as you go' is a winning formula for the energetically curious. Unpredictable weather and unreliable conditions underfoot are not considered legitimate 'opt out' excuses and a full complement of participants is the norm. It is very rewarding to watch their response (which often begins reticently) develop into free expression, born of the liberating confidence of understanding.

Several of the outings – the bus trip to Dysert O'Dea, the climb over the top of Mullaghmore Mountain, the traipse along the Flaggy Shore – are perennial favourites. But the one that can be guaranteed to engender the most enthusiastic response, both *en route* and afterwards in discussion, is the mass path hike to Gleninagh. This 10-kilometre clockwise circuit encompasses Cappanawalla Mountain. Beginning at the College at Newtown, the route goes south along the 'back road' to O'Lochlen's Cross (so named for the B&B owned by the venerable Burren family and the site of Patsy – last 'prince' of the Burren – O'Lochlen's house) and thence north through the Feenagh valley to upper Gleninagh and eventually to Gleninagh proper. It returns to the college along the main road and, ultimately, along the 'back road' again.

It is a significant undertaking, not so much for the distance, but for the variety of terrain encountered. More than half is on metalled road surface (no bother to youthful legs) but the middle section, through hoof-pocked fields, across stone walls and along a steep slippery track, presents a challenge, particularly for the more sedentary or urban-based students. In bad weather, it is definitely more of an endurance test than a pleasant hike. In fine weather, it is a joy.

Explaining the various styles of the ubiquitous stone walls is a regular source of discussion from the outset. The idea of laboriously enclosing an expanse of stark and apparently useless limestone outcrop with a flimsy-looking stone wall is a question that exercises the curiosity of most of the students from time to time. The emphasis is, however, on ecclesiastical matters. The mass path hike follows a morning lecture covering the late medieval and early modern period of Irish history which focuses particularly on the Penal Laws and the increasingly dire circumstances of the Irish in the first half of the nineteenth century, despite Catholic Emancipation.

Our walk takes in a number of locations which admirably illustrate the period. The first, not long after we have gone north up the Feenagh valley towards Gleninagh, is the ruin of Glenaraha chapel. The marquis of Buckingham built this 'mass house' for the Catholic parishioners of the Ballyvaughan valley in 1795, as the Penal Laws were easing. Emanating from Irish Catholic backgrounds (as invariably a number of students do), the notion of the Penal Laws comes as a shock. I always feel that such revelations must be tempered with the knowledge that religious discrimination in one form or another was a widespread phenomenon in Europe throughout this period. They do not need to be reminded of its insidious presence today.

Rathborney, a well-known ecclesiastical site a couple of hundred metres off the road to the left, is our next stop. This serene place usually elicits a respectful hush from the students, long enough at any rate for me to explain its important features: a fourteenth-century church ruin in a ringed enclosure which, as the name suggests, may have been a secular rath; dedicated perhaps to St John, who is linked with a holy well nearby; adorned with Gothic features such as a fine carved east window and protruding stone head; and replete with old graves and unmarked headstones. Questions from the students about the burial of Famine victims and unbaptised babies are commonplace but most queries relate to the continuing use of such a place for contemporary burials. Irish people take the practice for granted and pay little attention, for instance, to the appearance of fragments of human bone, turned up by gravediggers, on the surface of a new grave. Reaction from the students is rarely matter-of-fact; it may range from astonishment to disgust but it nonetheless illustrates an interesting cultural difference between our countries, a useful learning experience for the students.

A kilometre or two further north, we enter the fields where unfortunately all traces of the original mass path are gone, presumably eradicated some time ago by a bulldozer. A kilometre further, however, traces of the path are evident in a barely discernible ridge across a field and an irregularly filled section of the stone wall boundary. Once on the path, we can see its line in front extending onward through another stone wall and tracing a distant mark up the saddle at the head of the valley. This enigmatic path must have its origins in medieval times when the population of this remote valley regularly made their way from ring-fort cashels at Lismacteige, Lismacsheedy, Caherfeenagh and Caheranardros – homesteads of significant farmers – and the adjacent scatter of tenant bothies, to the little church in Gleninagh. If burials from the upper valley were also traditionally carried out in Gleninagh church, the path would certainly have been in constant use for centuries.

Glenaraha may have been the 'mass house' for the lower valley inhabitants well into the nineteenth century but would have been abandoned when the new church was built in Ballyvaughan in the nineteenth century. Burials, as we know, continued at Rathborney and in Gleninagh.

The view from the stone wall which links Cappanawalla with Aghaglinny at the Burren's northern buttress is one of the region's finest. The students, tired by the time they reach this point, habitually linger and soak it in. Even on a dull day, it is a feast for the eyes. The upland giving way suddenly and unexpectedly to the flat, fertile platform of Gleninagh stops each group in its tracks. Galway Bay, far below, with the Connemara coast beyond, resembles a wide river rather than a substantial bite out of Ireland's western seaboard. Everywhere one is surrounded by heritage: above on Aghaglinny height to the west we are overlooked by the inauguration site of the O'Lochlainn or O'Loghlen clan; directly below is the upright form of one of their last tower houses, occupied, we are told, by O'Loghlens into the nineteenth century; not far away the old quay from which, local tradition tells us, some of the Wild Geese (defeated leaders of the 1641 Rebellion and so named after their departure) left in the seventeenth century; close to the main Black Head road is our destination, the ruin of the little medieval church of Gleninagh surrounded by its oval-shaped sanctuary. It is clear from this elevated remove that the secluded, green 'island' of Gleninagh, hemmed in on both sides by rock outcrops, has been from the earliest times a desirable territory, occupied as much for its natural advantages as for its obvious fertility. Scanning the scene it is possible to pick out the remains of a ring fort and here and there crumbling ruined dwellings hidden in the encroaching scrub. A few unobtrusive modern bungalows emphasise the sense of continuity.

A cloud shadow on the sea materialises into a barque plying towards Gleninagh Pier to carry off the Earl of Ormonde; thin columns of smoke rise from a dozen stone and thatch cabins while black cattle like ants move towards the buaile, safe from wolves; exuberant peasants dressed in colourful woollen frieze garments, labouring under the weight of buttermilk containers, panting and bantering, stream up the steep hillside for the inauguration of their new chief; grieving coffin-bearers push close by along the mass path, the mourning cortege close behind, chanting their prayers in beautiful Irish.

As we return to the path, I remind the students that Gleninagh was an Irish-speaking community of 545 people before the Great Famine. Tom Donoghue, Gleninagh's last native Irish speaker, died at the turn of the second millennium, ending what must surely have been more than 1,500 years of linguistic continuity. What a pity it is lost.

The road is reached in less than half an hour and the students express both disappointment and relief. The church, our logical destination, beckons us down the narrow bóithrín and we linger there exchanging observations. We check the names on the headstones, recognising names familiar in the parish today. Many makeshift headstones, simple upright rocks, (surely Famine graves), punctuate the uneven ground of the little sanctuary. The castle, with its beautiful holy well, nearby fulachtaí fia and lime kiln, is just across the fields, but we leave that for another day. We have reached our destination by following in the footsteps of countless generations of devout inhabitants. For me, it is always a kind of pilgrimage.

My Burren Journey

George Cunningham

Since the early 1970s the Burren has been my second home, and I have come to love and respect its people, and its unique physical and cultural landscape. It has been my privilege to write and lecture on this region, hoping to inspire others with my love and respect for this small area of the mid-west of Ireland. During my school days at St Flannan's College, Ennis, County Clare, in the 1950s, the Burren was never mentioned, even in our geography classes. There were no local studies and there was no environmental consciousness at all. It was the same in all secondary schools of the time.

In the 1960s I was appointed principal of the National School at Coolderry near my hometown of Roscrea. My marriage in 1968 to Carmel gave me a partner who supported my local studies interest both in Roscrea and a little later in the Burren. This interest was further aided by access to collections in the public libraries and the Cistercian library at Mount St Joseph's monastery, Roscrea, County Tipperary.

I well remember our first extended visit to the Burren at Gregan's Castle Hotel, Ballyvaughan. The hotel is magnificently situated at the foot of the Corkscrew Hill. At that time there

The Burren, Ballyvaughan
© *Karin Funke*

were few contemporary books on the Burren – all I remember is Ennis man Gerry O'Connell's, *The Burren – A Guide*, notes by Professor Etienne Rynne, and E. K. Tratman's magisterial *The Caves of North-West Clare*. After our introduction to the Burren we returned there every year. We met others who were also interested in the region, like Dr Moss, who provided the Ordnance Survey six-inch maps of the Burren, and Betty O'Brien, who was then, like me, an amateur archaeologist (she later became a professional one).

Every day we spent in the Burren was a day of learning and discovery. We walked everywhere searching and finding, and immense was our joy when we stumbled across many unrecorded sites. I spent days drawing maps to help visitors find Poulnabrone Dolmen, Gleninsheen Wedge Tomb and the rath at Cahermore. Gradually these little maps evolved into a circular route from Gregan's Castle Hotel into Ballyvaughan, up to Aillwee Cave, on to Poulnabrone, Leamanagh Castle and Kilfenora (where the local Burren Centre opened in the 1970s) and back by Caherballykinvarga, Noughaval and Cahermacnaghten to Gregan's. This route later became the basis for my first book on the Burren, *Burren Journey*. Following its publication, helped by the late Seán White and Shannonside Tourism, I researched for a second book on the Burren, taking in the northern seaboard. The result was *Burren Journey West*.

After this I met kindred spirits, local man Michael Greene and his wife, Mary Hawkes Greene. Michael and Mary wished to attract a wider range of visitors to the Burren, who would appreciate its unique flora, landscape and heritage. Thus began the Burren Spring Conferences, which continue to this day. I will never forget one conference chaired by Professor Mary Ann Nevins Radzinowicz. In the middle of the conference the door burst open and this larger than life character, John O'Donohue (RIP), totally misreading the conference aims, berated us all that the conferences were only about money. He stormed out again, leaving us all completely bewildered. Later he was big enough to admit he was mistaken and apologise.

During preparations with Michael and Mary for the conferences, Michael told us of his dream of founding a college of art in the Burren. He wanted to create something different in his native place, something worthy of the great beauty of his Burren. To this end the Burren Trust was established, of which I was privileged to be a founding member. Also at this time the conferences on the Brehon Laws were initiated. The day the college became a reality was one of the proudest in the lives of those concerned. I am so pleased that Michael Greene lived to see this memorable day – for Michael was not to live long after this. Never will I forget that Sunday evening when Maryangela Keane phoned to break the news of Michael's death: Sunday 15 July 2001. He died, aged forty-four, while playing his beloved Gaelic football – such a heartbreak for his wife, Mary, and for his children, such a loss for Ballyvaughan and the nearby villages. The Burren was deprived of its greatest champion.

At the following Burren conference in March 2002, the opening evening was devoted to Dreaming the Dream, a tribute to Michael. We announced the proposal to erect a stained glass window in his memory in his parish church, St John the Baptist in Ballyvaughan. Artist Manus Walsh designed the window and it was crafted by Aria Stained Glass Studios in Galway. Michael bequeathed a proud legacy which we can but try to emulate. I certainly am proud to have been his friend and collaborator in promoting the best interests of the Burren.

Remembering John O'Donohue

Lelia Doolan

'Tis unknown the people he helped!' a friend said to me the other day. She went on to tell how John's friendship had helped her through a time of great sorrow.

I never meet anyone who knew John but we immediately start talking about him. Talking over the occasions of chance meetings or evenings together, phone calls, jokes, reflective moments of calm enjoyment over a pint or a glass of whiskey.

So there will be many people reading this with their own precious memories of the rare bird that he was and, like me, they'll be missing his large hug, his great rumbling laughter and his clear, wild, wise head.

Around the villages along the coast, the sea below Fanore and the fields above Black Head, the elements must miss him too. He exulted in the fierce gales that roamed the mountains. These were his acres to pace across, clearing his thoughts – just as the roads around his home in Conamara must miss his running stride.

The breathing life of nature was home to him. It was there in every bit of his character. His writing recounted its ever-changing face smiling on him, but he also felt its storms stirring up hidden forces and finding their echo in human upheavals. He understood that our powers can be benign or malevolent by turns and he caught and somehow found a way to balance those mighty contradictions and nuances on the tip of his tongue, on the tip of his digging pen. He encouraged and suffered nature, family and his home valley to nurture and teach him, to fire his grand explorer's intellect and to liberate his soul.

And of course he knew not just its faces and moods but also its stories. He was druid and priest, folklorist and storyteller. The names and tales of fields and their boundaries were as familiar and evocative as the names of friends and neighbours, their history and the echo of lives long gone. The deserted collection of homesteads above his family's house is a place of plaintive beauty and mystery in the lives it had borne and witnessed. In him, it must have fuelled an awareness of morsels of overlooked human history, the harshness of life, its tragic brevity and the tough undaunted spirits of the dispossessed.

You couldn't spend time in John's company, hear him 'do a blast' as he called giving a talk, or read his books but you would be enriched with some new insight – or several new insights. Eloquence is a poor word to describe the quality of his deceptively simple time-bombs of ideas. They reverberate long afterwards. They were immediately intelligible, always enjoyable and pointed to a spirituality that seemed to be possible for the church but somehow absent from it. People will remember his voice as a resonant, uncluttered Clareman's voice, sometimes lingering over a syllable or a telling phrase for emphasis but moving steadily on without hesitation and mercifully free from any clerical form of 'improved' elocution.

It seemed as if his fine intelligence and self-discipline had enabled him to burn off much unnecessary detail in order to seek the core of a thing and to work towards leaner forms. At the same time the expression of his ideas was always richly tactile. It was woven with a host of allusions to poets, painters, philosophers and local storytellers. To read any single section of *Anam Cara*, *Eternal Echoes* or *Divine Beauty* is to be awestruck by the breadth of his interests, his knowledge of art, of language, of the down-to-earth challenges of daily life. His two books of poetry and his magnificent *Benedictus* are testaments to his own deepening power as a poet.

He was keenly aware of the passing of time, so that there was never enough to stretch to the huge number of projects he had in mind to undertake, such as writing a philosophy of landscape; working with a study group to analyse Ireland at the crossroads; using Hegel's method to explore some thresholds in Irish memory and history; writing a novel about the Famine as the crucifixion of Irish consciousness; or 'continuing to excavate the territories of poetry', one of the pursuits he most valued. The publication of a collection of his essays will one day make a valuable contribution to modern philosophical thought.

We will miss him as a true friend and a good listener (once you caught his attention!). He had an ability to tune completely in to a need or a hurt and pay it its complete due; people bereaved or cast down were comforted simply by his presence. I remember once when a young friend of mine was going through a tough time and I asked John whether he might have time to come for a walk with us. We went off walking over bog and lakeland in Conamara; not much was said, but I know that John's attentiveness and his few words about the place and its history diverted and relieved the young man's heart. Many such stories are recounted since his death and I am sure there will be many more.

In *Anam Cara* he tells the story of the loneliness of a friend who was studying in Germany and how, in the winter, after a bad dose of 'flu, he became unbearably homesick, so much so that one day he decided to let the loneliness have its way. He sat down and let it flow through him. He wept and wept, facing all the loneliness he had kept hidden. In facing and befriending it and feeling its depth, something shifted and became free in him so that he was never again lonely in Germany. I suspect that this student friend was John himself and that the story is a model for the way in which he generously opened himself to situations and people.

I will miss all of those great qualities of presence: the sight of his swiftly approaching smiling form, the compassionate soaring archway to the divine that he imagined for us, the playfulness and puckish mad humour that broke out in the blink of an eye. He'll be present in all the places his great spirit inhabited for as long as we have spirit to inhabit them too.

The Harvesters of the Sea

Sarah Poyntz

The currach goes back a long way in our maritime history. The Brehon Laws of the old Gaelic system, long before the Norman invaders of the twelfth century, mention them and give the honour-price of the boatbuilders. They describe the traditional currach: a vessel covered with hide and built with a frame and ribs of hazel, ash, oak, willow, the wood selected according to availability locally. The animal hide was tarred and made sea-worthy. Many of the Clare currachs were built in Inis Oírr, the nearest Aran Island to the Clare coast, but unlike the Aran currachs, they had a raised stern to give better manoeuvrability in shallow waters and in a following sea.

In the early nineteenth century, during the Napoleonic Wars, Royal Navy officers stationed along the coast in Martello towers modified the Clare currach. Tarred canvas replaced the animal hide and a double-gunwale frame was incorporated, thus lengthening the craft.

Captain J. Frazier, one of the officers concerned, wrote in the *Clare Journal* of 1822, 'it is perfectly astonishing with what courage and bravery these hardy men will continue in this tempestuous ocean … I had no idea that men could be found to venture themselves in so "frail a bark" amidst the tremendous waves of the Atlantic ocean.' Captain Frazier was probably stationed in the Martello tower on Finavarra, which can be seen from Ballyvaughan, Gleninagh and along the coast.

John Millington Synge described his journey in a currach from Inis Meáin to Inis Oírr in *The Aran Islands*:

It was a four-oared curagh [*sic*], and I was given the last seat so as to leave the stern for the man who was steering with an oar, worked at right angles to the others by an extra thole-pin in the stern gunnel ... The shower had passed over and the wind had fallen, but large, magnificently brilliant waves were rolling down on us at right angles to our course ... The curagh seemed to leap and quiver with the frantic terror of a beast until the wave passed behind or fell with a crash beside the stern.

It was in this racing with the waves that our chief danger lay. If the wave could be avoided, it was better to do so, but if it overtook us while we were trying to escape and caught us on the broadside, our destruction was certain. I could see the steersman quivering with the excitement of his task, for any error in his judgement would have swamped us.

I enjoyed the passage. Down in this shallow trough of canvas that bent and trembled with the motion of the men, I had a far more intimate feeling of the glory and the power of the waves than I have ever known in a steamer.

Synge caught the very essence of the currach, frail but with unexpected strength.

The Burren villages had their brave men and women but none had more than little Gleninagh, situated between Ballyvaughan and Fanore. Today we can sit on Gleninagh's harbour wall and imagine it when anything up to fourteen currachs put out to sea when the day was full of light or when darkness lay soft on land and sea, when the outward trip was sure but the return was never certain. Off the oarsmen went, skimming the surface water in their light craft, finding places to fish, loading the currachs if they were in luck and navigating them back to harbour.

There was a time in the Famine when they were unable to fish, for each currach 'required three men to row effectively, and these should row, while fishing, about ten miles. This length of rowing in our very rough seas required strength and agility, which had fled from the skin-and-bones frame of poor fishermen ...'[1]

The Gleninagh people fished for mackerel and herring, with cod, ling and haddock caught in early spring. The fish were sold on Gleninagh Pier and sent to Clare and Limerick. They were also sent to Galway when it was evident that the men from the Claddagh in Galway had not been fishing, for it was known that there was a market there. With the advent of the railways in the nineteenth century the fish were sent to Ardrahan to the train station and transported to Dublin for the early afternoon market – fresh fish sold in the capital the same day they were caught off Gleninagh.

In the nineteenth century, visitors were rowed out to view the cliff scenery and to explore the caves. This was good for the fishermen when the fishing was poor, but it was very dangerous and only possible in good weather, and there were many drownings of visitors and crews.

Lobster and crab were rarely caught commercially until

---

1   Father Meehan speaking about conditions during the Great Famine of 1848 as quoted in *The Traditional Boats of Ireland*, edited by Criostóir Mac Cárthaigh, 2008.

the twentieth century. It required a two-man currach – room had to be made for the twenty or so lobster pots, which were usually made of hazel. Apart from the crustaceans, there is no commercial fishing in the area now: Patsy Mullins goes out every day to attend his lobster and crab pots, just like his father before him, and his catch is sold every Saturday morning at the Ballyvaughan weekly market.

Change

Sarah Poyntz

The ever-whirling wheel
Of change.

Edmund Spenser: *The Faerie Queen*

Like the rest of Ireland, the Burren villages of Ballyvaughan, Bell Harbour, Gleninagh and Fanore have changed over many years. Their inhabitants are the witnesses of these changes. Without their record, nurtured by memory and experience, we would find it exceedingly difficult, if not impossible, to quantify and detail the changes wrought within the communities.

All four villages are close to the sea with their common hinterland of fertile fields, rocky spaces and gentle, stony hills. Ballyvaughan, Gleninagh and Bell Harbour lie snug in their valleys, as does part of Fanore, while its other part is crested above the Atlantic. The physical changes to the environment include roads, buildings, construction, walls and land reclamation. To travel from place to place, today's inhabitants, except farmers, no longer use the old roads, the Green Roads (originally called Bóithríní na Gorta, famine roads). They use the macadamed roads, although there is little change in these – still badly surfaced and bumpy.

New types of fences, even pillars, to define property limits have appeared. The old drystone walls (especially those of layered single stones) have in a few cases been replaced by wooden fences or walls of cement blocks, sometimes faced with stone. Land is reclaimed either to add to farmland or to make sites for new houses and buildings. Great machines lift the huge limestone pavements, tip them into other machines where they are ground down to fist-size stones for construction foundations. Hardly a place is inaccessible to this type of work, made possible by the turn of a key in ignition or the easy movement of a lever. It is a change from the work of our common ancestors who, before the Egyptians constructed the Giza Pyramids, built Newgrange in County Meath from mighty rocks transported many kilometres. Even the dolmens, wedge tombs and forts scattered throughout the Burren and, much later for the most part, the small ruined churches and the large abbey ruins are evidence of physical human might. Today we can but wonder at such extraordinary human strength.

Then there is the change of function: houses or buildings being used for purposes other than their former or original use; for example, what was once the post office in Ballyvaughan is now a gift shop, Lillimar. Claire's Restaurant was transformed into a pharmacy and then a take-away. Modifications and additions also bring change. Logue's Pub in Ballyvaughan had a Bed and Breakfast section added by the previous owners, Eddie and Maureen O'Brien. It could be said that it has returned to its original use, since it was once a well-known hotel.

All these activities change the physical look of the villages and their surroundings. People reared in the villages return sometimes after a long absence to find their 'own' place changed. These operations also change other aspects of the Burren in that they decrease the age-old shelters of the region's wildlife and diminish the profusion of its flora.

While most inhabitants of the three villages descend from families long settled there, other people marry in and, of course, there are the blow-ins – those who have no connection with the area but who choose to settle there whether for work or retirement. In addition, people born and reared in the villages often leave, either to secure jobs unavailable in their area or for other reasons.

Perhaps the greatest change of all is that from human hands, feet, backs and sheer muscle to machinery. Motorised vehicles – cars, vans, lorries, trucks, tractors – now transport people, animals and goods. In the early twentieth century, the inhabitants used muscle, hands and arms on farms and in trades, their backs to load and unload heavy items, their feet to walk the distances. The old boats that plied the sea from Connemara and Galway bringing turf and goods are no more. Specialised machines and tools have replaced strength and force.

When we examine these villages of our beautiful Burren today, letting our eyes move from sea to hill, from rocky field to green pasturage where lovely herds lie quietly, we are shocked to recall that we would be bereft of all this but for the farming habits of people long ago. They decimated the woods which anchored the soil, making inevitable the erosion which occurred over time.

When we stand with our backs to the sea and examine the terrain of this western outpost of Ireland and Europe, these Burren coastal villages, remembering what the people of this region say, 'Our next parish west is Boston', we notice the valleys and, dominating them, the Burren hills or mountains. Then the stones, the mighty limestone rocks, the great slabs of calcareous pavements not haphazardly scattered but forming the very structure, the very innards of the land, strike us. We wonder at its power, its strangeness, its lack of trees, and its seeming inhospitality. We wonder at the survival of its inhabitants. How did they farm, for farm they did, such a land?

Then we turn towards the sea, the powerful Atlantic, which washes these limestone shores and smashes in the frequency of its storms the seemingly impregnable and fortress-like coast. How did the farmers of the sea, its fishermen, live?

We know from history that their ancestors survived foreign rule, the often vicious landlord system, famine, emigration, wars against the foreign invader (almost every half century over 800 years), and then civil war, but how did they survive on this land when it finally became their own?

Here the people tell their own story, mainly from the 1950s onwards but with flashbacks to earlier times.

Oisín and Niamh[1]

Sure it was all mainly cereal farming until nearly the 1980s. During the Second World War, there was the compulsory tillage. There had to be, to keep the country fed. Each farmer had his quota and had to keep to it. It was very strict but there was no trouble really. We all knew it had to be that way for the

---

1 The couple I spoke to wished to remain anonymous, so I have given them the names of two of the ancient characters from the Fenian Cycle who were specially connected to Munster.

country to survive. Otherwise there'd be famine. Most of the crops, the wheat and barley, were sold to Coens of Gort. Before that, the barley was sold to Persse's Distillery in Galway – that was Lady Gregory's family. They were landlords, not very good ones by all accounts, but she was different, a good woman, married to Gregory of Coole Park. She wrote and was in with all the other writers of the time – that'd be way back now.

There was another crop too, the sugar beet. From the 1940s, from the end of October to near Christmas time, you'd see the beet lining all the roads here about, great mounds of it waiting to be collected by trucks from the sugar factory in Tuam, County Galway. The sugar-beet growing all stopped in the twenty-first century. It was great while it lasted because you'd get the payment just before Christmas. That'd be a big help.

Then there was the hay. 'Twas needed for cattle feed, essential back then 'cos there was no silage at all. Most farmers, if they could, kept a few cattle, some for themselves for the milk. The hay-saving was in the summer. 'Tis very anxious you'd be for the good weather to reap the hay. It used to be done with scythes, and they say before that with reaping hooks. Everybody helped, all the neighbours would come and then you'd go to help them when it was their turn. There was no payment whatever. It was called meitheal, which means work-sharing without payment or wages. Each man brought his own scythe and he didn't like to lend it to anyone else. After the cutting and drying, the hay would have to be raked up into 'troms' or 'trams' as they were called – cocks of hay. Sheds were rare in those days. Sometimes some of the women helped but they were mostly busy with the meals. Everyone had to be fed. 'Twas the meals that kept us going. There'd be home-baked brown and white soda bread, ham, tomatoes, tea and stout. That'd be brought to the fields and then after all the work at the end of the day there'd be a meal in the house with a big basket of potatoes put in the centre of the table for everyone to help himself and there'd be a big plateful of food for each, cabbage and whatever.

There'd be fun too after getting in the hay; music – someone would always strike up the fiddle or the concertina and there'd be singing and a bit of dancing too and maybe a few stories. Some would stay overnight and the trestle bed would be pulled out for them. Yes, they'd sleep in the one bed, so tired they'd drop off at once. Later the machinery came but the tractors didn't come until the 1960s, not here, they didn't. They changed everything. Then the work became easier and the farmer was able to do it himself so the meitheal died out but sure even still you'd always get a helping hand if you were stuck. Of course it'd be different over in the east where there'd be the real big farms.

To be sure, nearly everyone had a few cows for the milk and the butter. You'd take the milk down to Ballyvaughan to the creamery over by Clareville. They'd skim it there and then you'd take back the skimmed milk for the calves. Before you'd take it down you'd keep back enough for the family and to give to people who mightn't have cows. No one ever ran short of milk. 'Twas given freely. Some people used to put a pinch of salt in it beforehand. 'Twas a kind of custom in places around, a piseog I suppose. It was right hard to keep the evening milk fresh in the hot weather. So wherever there was a bit of a river like over Fanore way, the Caher river, and down in the valley, the bit of the Rathborney river that's over-ground (most of it is underground), you could put the evening milk down in them and then take it up in the morning. It was fierce heavy lifting it up. It was good when the creamery came because you'd get the money for the milk just before Christmas. 'Twould come in handy then, I can tell you. The women did most of the milking. Some would be milking sixteen or seventeen cows, in rain or shine. A few would be able to do their milking in a shed but not many.

Some people walked their cattle to the Gort Fair (24kms). They would start about four in the morning. Some of them might stop on the way with relatives for the night. The relations would give them a field for the cattle and they'd be off again the next morning.

A local man round Bell Harbour way used to sell cows and calves. Once he was showing some calves to a farmer and his wife when they noticed bald ends to the calves' tails and exclaimed, 'They've got the scour.'

'Sure of course they have the scour. Haven't all the animals around belonging to the big farmers got it? Don't I have it myself? – You'd know if I showed you the tail of my shirt!'

Nearly everyone kept one and often two or more pigs. You'd kill a pig in October or when there was an 'r' in the month, and on a rising moon, between the new moon and the first quarter, and on a Friday and then again in the spring. We used to try to keep the children away for that. We'd have a neighbour on the look-out for them walking home from school. We had a kind of system of hanging out tea towels high up on bushes so the neighbour would see them and get the message. You'd get the message by the number of tea towels. 'Twas a kind of morse code. We can laugh now about it when there are phones, mobile phones, computers and all that, but it was real handy back then. The meat would be put in two big barrels full of brine and salt to last till the next killing. Parcels of the meat would be given to neighbours, even the head and all the innards were used.

Everything was shared – the neighbours would do the same when they killed their pig. Nothing was wasted. Later all the women would come to make the putógs (puddings) and the children would help then too. There'd be a big pot of boiling water on the fire. You had to turn the intestines inside out to clean them. Then you'd turn them back again to fill them with a mixture of the pig's blood, oatmeal and all kinds of spices. I remember ginger and nutmeg. Then they'd be tied in a circle with a knot and put on the handle of a brush to be dipped in the boiling water to cook them. The putógs were regarded as a great delicacy and were considered to be a non-meat dish so could be, and were, eaten on Fridays, the day of abstinence for Roman Catholics back then. Very often a braon (drop) accompanied the meal of putógs like a scáiltín (hot whiskey) or a poitín.

Great care had to be taken of the sow before farrowing. Each member of the family was fully instructed in the details of the birth. Very often the sow was brought into the kitchen and put in a kind of enclosure so that the other jobs of the house could be done. After the birth, the sow and the banbhs (piglets) would be moved out into the cró muice (pigsty) and allowed into an adjacent field that had plenty of greenery and special weeds. This was to make up for any deficiency in the sow's milk.

The people of the villages used the markets of Ennistymon, Gort, and of course Ballyvaughan. The last of these, held every Thursday, was very popular and was usually crowded with horses, asses, carts, produce of every kind, all grown locally. Thursday too was the day the boats came in from Connemara laden with turf and often with poitín hidden cleverly underneath. John Burke used to come in from Fanore with the Carrucans, and people'd come from Bell Harbour and Ucht Máma and all over. Unlike the markets of today there was a great deal of barter, potatoes swapped for turf maybe. The public houses, opened early, were full and did a good trade. There were few chickens or other fowl for sale because the rearers had their regular customers. Keanes of Gort came to buy and weigh the wool, although some wool was kept and brought to Ennistymon to be oiled. The old weighing machine is still there between O'Loghlen's Whiskey Pub and Mooney-Hynes.

Then there was old Gundy O'Loghlen (Thady O'Loghlen), the blacksmith. He'd be shoeing horses, asses, fixing ploughs. He was a good blacksmith. All the children would gather to watch him at work.

There was one man who came to the markets and fairs to sell his produce. He sold it quickly and then went to the pub, where he spent the rest of the day. One time he was about to set off home after dark when he noticed a garda watching. The man had no light for his ass and cart. He undid the ass and tied it to the back of the cart, got between the shafts himself and pulled the cart back home himself.

Sheep were also kept. Tommy Fahy walked a flock of sheep from Bell Harbour to Gort (about 18kms) in the 1940s. The snow was high and heavy on the roads. It was a terrible journey. Many farmers also kept goats. The kids were kept in the dark and fed prátaí (potatoes), they were treated the way calves for veal are now, then they were sold to regular customers. Sometimes they were sent up the mountain to mix with the wild goats. People said they were the best animals for keeping the scrub down because they ate everything, cattle being much more selective in what they eat. Unease was expressed that there had been recent culling of the wild goats. These animals gave a sense of confidence because they could be milked if things ever got really bad. It was also said that gangs from Limerick were capturing the kids and sending them to English restaurants. Cappanawalla seems especially bereft of these creatures. The late John McNamara of Fanore would be very upset, for he had a care for them.

You'd have to have a fine day for bringing home the turf, and people from Ballyvaughan walked to the bog, up the Corkscrew, past Gregan's. Others might have their own bit of bog for the turf. They'd all have their food for the day and a bottle of tea. Later some people would go on their bikes, but they had no tyres as 'twas very hard to get tyres in those days and they were very dear. The children would be kept off school for a week and it was hard work all day in the sun. You had to take about 25 centimetres (10 inches) off the top of the bog first, then you'd use the sleán, which had a small cutting edge on one side. You'd cut sods of about 30 centimetres (12 inches) long and 15 wide (6 inches) with the sleán. You had to bend over all the time. There was a special wheelbarrow for the cut turf. It had a flat body and a front, no sides. And there were little asses to carry the turf in baskets on each side. Some men used to make these baskets. Mick Carrucan was a great basket-maker when he lived out in Fanore; Christy Irwin made fine baskets too. It was wonderful, that generation of men and women – they had all kinds of skills as they always did the work themselves. They had no choice as there wasn't the money to pay anyone and people took a pride in what they did and did it right, because it had to last. The turf had to be spread out to dry and when you brought it home you'd build it up against the wall, a reek of turf it was called, and you'd cover it with grass and bushes – there was no such thing as plastic in those days.

They say the bog and turf is great for preserving things. I know the archaeologists found all sorts of ancient things in the bogs, even very old butter. Now that's something.

There was hardly a house that wasn't thatched and each man did his own with maybe a bit of help from a neighbour. We all know the old saying, 'Ní hé lá na gaoithe lá na scoilb', 'the windy day is not the day for scollops', so not the day for thatching. The scollops were the hazel rods used to keep the straw in place and they were cut in the hazel woods. They had to be cut in November when the sap was down, and were cleaned and made ready by the fire during the winter before the thatching. They'd need to be about a metre long and they'd have a point at each end. About every five years you'd have to thatch to keep it in good order, though you might have to do around the chimney more often. Some of the houses were 500 years old. Some people preferred the straw because they could grow it themselves and it looked better on the houses. The outhouses could be thatched in reeds and some people thatched the top of the reeks (or ricks) of hay to keep it dry. Each household had to grow its own straw, that'd be the straw from either wheat or oats. It had to be reaped by hand because when the machines came you couldn't use the straw after them – they cut it too sharp.

The hazel was a godsend for thatching work and it was also used for the scuttles, the baskets for the cooked potatoes. There were special containers to hold the straw for thatching. They were made of plaited straw or osiers and were shield-shaped so the straw fitted into them like a glove on a hand. The whole roof would have an awful lot of streaks or bundles of straw, that is the length and width of straw that a man could manage on his own. When the straw was laid on the roof then it had to be fixed firmly with the hazel rods which had to be pliant of course. Then there was the special tool for the thatching called a scolb tuí, a kind of looped stick for securing the thatch. You'd hear no sound at all with thatch – you'd not know if it was raining – and this made things nice and quiet. A good few people put bluestone on the thatch – it made the whole roof all gold and it would kill any fungus.

Things came a bit easy with the machines. We didn't know how hard those times were. You just accepted the life you had and got on with it. Then we were self-sufficient. We ate what we grew and grew what sheltered us and we had the fun of the stories, the dances, the music and songs. We made it all ourselves, the fun, the work, and the nourishment. We weren't always wanting to know the time, always looking at the clock. I'll tell you a story now that'll give you a laugh. Out Gleninagh way there was a couple, Mary and Johnnie. Their children were all gone away from them. They had a big clock up on the wall. One day Mary said to Johnnie, 'That clock is getting very dusty up there.' So Johnnie put an old skirt of Mary's over the clock.

They used to have regular visits from the priest so he came one evening and said, 'I can't stay very long this evening. What time is it now?'

'Ah, sure look up there under Mary's skirt!' said Johnnie.

A Day in the Life of a Farmer's Wife

Mary Keane

I had a good few boyfriends before I married but I wasn't at ease with any of them. Then I met P.J. and I felt at ease with him so I married him. That was in 1958. We went away for four days and we never took another break for twenty-five years, when we went to Rosslare to celebrate our silver wedding. We went up the Barrow River on a barge. Years later we went to America to see P.J.'s two brothers and three sisters. P.J. used to wonder if their houses were as good as they said, emigrants tending to boast a bit, but they were. All of them went to night classes and got themselves qualified. When asked their reason for leaving Ireland they replied, 'We had nothing there.'

P.J. had his brother, Michael, and his mother, Nanny, living with him and I didn't think anything of going to live among them. We all got on together, all of us busy. There was always something to be done, to be attended to.

We got up at 5 a.m. every morning. The fire had to be started for the little breakfast. Everyone had bread and tea. The men went off to check up on the animals while I checked on the fowl. We kept chickens, hens and a cock, geese, ducks and turkeys. Later when the light was better, the times of doing things changed according to the season and the amount of light. Milking had to be done whether it was rain or shine. There were no sheds in those days except one small one for a sick animal. I had a name for each cow like Carron and Kilshanny. I'd often, when milking, lean my head against the cow's flank and the cow would turn her head and lick me. They were very quiet and gentle. They never panicked but stood quite still and calm. They knew their milkers well.

Then I carried in the buckets of milk and emptied them into special containers. These were kept scrupulously clean by scouring them with boiling water. There were four of them, each one with its own registered number. Two were used each day and were taken by ass and cart down to the creamery depot in Ballyvaughan, near Clareville. There the cream was taken off and the separated milk was brought back to the farm and fed to the calves. This task took place only in spring and summer, the calves being born in March or April. For the winter, two cows and their calves were kept to give milk so there was no shortage of it. People who had no cows were given milk by those who had them.

After the milking, I fed the hens, geese, ducks and turkeys and their young. I gave them boiled potatoes and meal, mostly oats. They had to be fed often, like babies. I fed the pigs all the leftovers. We kept three pigs, one for the family, two for selling. Any surplus fowl were mostly sold at the Ballyvaughan market before Christmas. In winter, I had to feed the cattle their hay. The hay was fixed to a rope, called a barth, which I slung over my back and carried out to the field. I gave each cow her hay, taking care that none dropped to the ground where it would be trampled and wasted. Then I brought the rope back and hung it up.

At about 11 a.m. all of us, after about four hours' work, would have our big breakfast, brown homemade bread, boiled eggs, tea. After that, there would be more work in the fields according to the season, haymaking, cutting turf on the bog, cutting hazel for the thatch, repairing stone walls. I would wash the clothes by hand, do the afternoon milking (this had to be done before the light went) and prepare the dinner, which was eaten at about 2 p.m. There was no counting of what was cooked but the table was always set for eight, excluding the children who were either too small to go to the table or later on were at school. Any neighbour who wanted could join the family for this dinner. Passers-by could always drop in. That was the custom in those days. The food was wholesome: razor fish, bacon, cabbage, beetroot, rhubarb, apples and blackberries in season, wild strawberries (served with sugar and cream), pancakes with butter, brown bread, potatoes, milk and eggs.

After the dinner, I baked the bread. I used a three-legged pot. I piled the hot coals on top of the pot and all around it. The coals were still hot after the dinner. The pot was called gréithe from the Irish. Then I'd finish off any work remaining and then it was the time for feeding the dogs and cats.

Often after dark, the neighbours would drop in and Nanny (my mother-in-law) would read the news from the newspaper. Nanny could speak, read and write English and Irish. Most people spoke Irish all the time. She would often insert a spicy bit of news, made up by herself, into her newspaper reading. This caused great laughter and fun and the listeners would be always on the alert for it. People from all over our valley came to Nanny with their letters in English. Then she would read them or translate them into Irish and then read them out.

One of the joys of country life in the long, dark winters was to be with neighbours and especially the older people around the fireside. There would be chat about local doings, the crops, the weather, the price of cattle, the births and marriages. It was a treat to watch the men filling their pipes with tobacco around the open fire. The young people sat on the hob, a seat beside the fire. They loved to hear the older generation telling stories, sometimes fairy stories, and they'd watch very closely when card games were played.

These were special times, and even more special was Christmas time. Like other mothers and fathers, we went to town very early in the morning to do the Christmas shopping in the horse and cart and later in the car. The children waited all day for our homecoming. 'Bringing of the Christmas' it was called. They watched the boxes being brought in and stored away until Christmas Eve. Then no window blinds would be drawn down so that the light would shine out to show the way to Mary and Joseph, for Mary to have her baby. The oldest or youngest person in the house lit the candles – there was a candle in each window. Everyone knelt down and said a prayer at each candle, a prayer for God's protection until the next Christmas. The Christmas log was brought in and placed at the back of the fire in the open hearth. It sent out warmth to make our toast for Christmas Eve. The bread was stuck at the end of a long wire fork and held against the glowing turf.

Christmas morning was lovely. We, like the other parents, walked with our children to 6 a.m. mass. Candles shed their light from every window of every farmhouse as we walked in the dark. The lighted church welcomed all, and of course the crib was very special for the young ones. Those times were never forgotten by anyone, grown-up or child.

There was no electricity for a long time so oil lamps or

candles were used. People mostly went to bed early because there was work to be done from 5 a.m. the next morning.

THE CHILDHOOD OF BREDA MORAN (NÉE KEANE)

Up our way, in Lismacteige, there were plenty of people: the Vaughans, Cahalans, Howards, Deelys, Donoghues and ourselves. I grew up in the 1960s. We, my brothers, sisters, and myself, walked the mass road to school and to mass every Sunday too. The road went by J. J. Keane's house, and then out by the school – it's the Burren Way now. We all had jobs to do, and we used to look after the goats. We had six goats and we used to sell the kids in town for Christmas. We had regular customers for them and we could keep the money we got for them. Otherwise we hardly knew what money was, though my mother would slip us some now and again. Come the end of August the nannies would dry out and we'd let them off up the mountain. Then when the spring came, the time for them to have their babies, we'd go up the mountain for them with my father. He'd have a bag of meal and prataí in his pocket. He'd rattle that and our goats would come back to us because they were used to being hand-fed. One year, and I remember it well, there was one little kid left over. My father said, 'Cook it for the dinner.' My mother wasn't happy about that but she cooked it anyway. But all of us children refused to go in to eat dinner. We all sat on the wall outside and we wouldn't budge. My father was going mad and my mother kept saying, 'I told you they wouldn't eat it.' We stayed on strike. We couldn't eat it because we'd played with it and had given it a name. When my father was gone out of the house my mother cooked burgers for us and brought us in for our dinner.

My mother would never let us be in the house when a pig was killed. She'd warn Mary Ann Vaughan and Mary would meet us after school and take us to her place and give us dinner. Later of course we'd help making the putógs.

I remember one summer's day we took my Uncle Michael's air bed – it was for an extra guest to sleep on. Well, we nicked the bed and we took it off down to the river, the Rathborney, and went floating off on it. Later we sneaked it back but that evening Christy Cahalan came up to the house and he asked, 'Where did they get that lovely boat they had on the river today?' Sure we were nearly killed.

Then my mother had a bicycle. When she'd be milking way behind the house I used to be the watch-out standing at the corner. I had to watch her all the time. My brothers would steal the bicycle out of the car house and they'd be off down the field on it. I'd have to give them the word when she was near finished.

Halloween was great. We used to set the table and leave the front door open for the poor souls, in case any of them came back. The table would be left like that all night and the front door unlocked. Then we used to have apples hanging from the rafters which you would try to catch in your mouth, or you'd dip your head in a basin and try to get a penny.

We had a very free childhood. Mother would let us off in the morning and it might be dark before she'd start thinking, 'Well, where are they?' Then she'd blow on a policeman's whistle she had and we'd know that the potatoes were on. She used to cook a big dinner in the evenings. As soon as we heard the whistle, we would have twenty minutes to get home. My father would hear the whistle way up the mountain. We had a great system with tea towels across the valley with the Vaughans – it was about half a mile across. If the Vaughans wanted a lift to mass, they'd put a tea towel on a certain bush. We'd know then that they wanted to go to mass with us. Sometimes when I was a teenager I'd have a tiff with my mother. So I'd go across to Mary Ann Vaughan and she'd always say, 'Go hang these tea towels on the line.' Then my mother would know where I was.

We got electricity about 1959 and in the winter we all played cards every night and Mother and Father taught us to dance. They taught us 'sets' and the 'Walls of Limerick'. My father was always afraid that if we didn't know how to dance we'd be wallflowers. My father reckoned that they, the boys, sent an ugly-looking fellow to ask you first. If you were pleasant to him then they'd all ask you. It was very important never to say 'No'. The card games we played were called 'combs and outs', twenty-five and forty-five. 'Combs and outs' was also played down in Greene's bar in Ballyvaughan.

Every Saturday evening Father would cut hair, ours and anybody's. All the neighbours would come and the Woods family too. It was the night of the baths too. Mother would put us in and after our bath she'd put on our nightdresses. Then my Uncle Michael would rag our hair with torn flour bags so that we'd have ringlets.

We didn't often go to the village but we went on sports day or for races. They used to have races at Newtown Castle and I heard they used to have plays in the 1950s. They'd come for a week and do a different play each night.

We used to like having a drive in the car. I think my father had a Model T first and I remember a Ford Anglia. We'd drive over to my grandfather, my mother's father, in Kilshanny on Stephen's Day. There'd be a big box full of clothes. We'd all be trying on dresses. We could wear my cousins' clothes because we didn't go to the same schools and no one would know in Ballyvaughan. In that way, we had loads of clothes, all hand-me-downs.

My grandmother had great Irish but then it died out in the area. But there was the Irish Tree on the way in to Ballyvaughan. It's there still. That tree was the signal in the old days to stop speaking Irish. It had to be English from then on because you were near the village and it was forbidden to speak Irish. 'Twas the opposite on the way back. When you reached it then the Irish flowed.

There were superstitions too. If you washed your face when the sun was on the grass, you'd get rid of your freckles. On New Year's Day, it was bad luck for a woman to go out. Once my mother sent me off for a bottle of milk. I fell on the ice coming home. My father went mad and said, 'I told you not to be sending a girl out of the house on New Year's Day. What was wrong with you and two lads in the house?'

Then we had a man, Billy Barrett, working for my father. Billy was a bit slow and the lads set him up one time. Billy was mad about the girl who worked in the shop where the T-junction is now. The lads bought a pair of pink knickers for the girl's birthday and they persuaded Billy to give her the present. She went mad when she opened it and saw the big pair of pink bloomers.

We used to have Americans over for holidays and Agnes Swift came. Her people were related to Jonathan Swift. She knew my aunt in Boston. She used to take photos of us. She ran a library and every September they'd get new books. So she'd send us the old ones and she took out a subscription for us to the *National Geographic*. We used to like reading that.

A Burren Upbringing

Liam Glynn

I try to recall the moment as a child that this 'place of stone' was born in my consciousness. There was a stone that my mother and I would religiously pause at every day on the way to the kitchen garden for cabbage and new potatoes for that day's dinner. Indeed, those moments each day had all the reverence of a religious ceremony as she urged me to listen quietly to a nearby birdsong or examine the spring gentian or orchid that had made its home in the shelter of that stone: God's own handiwork revealed on earth. It does not surprise me to this day that the Burren draws into it people searching for the 'other' in their own lives.

It may have been the numerous small circular stone structures that dotted my childhood landscape that became the fortified castles of imagined battles. My mother, grandmother and generations before had used these goat botháns, to milk and to house the newly born goats while their mothers spent their days grazing the rich mountain flora. *Capra hircus* or 'the poor man's cow' occupies a special place in the lived memory of Burren people. My grandmother always claimed earnestly that it 'was the goat that rose us from poverty', which is not surprising given this animal's marvellous fecundity and the rich diet that was available year round. The goat has been a vital part of the economy of the Burren since first brought here by Neolithic peoples. The distinctive flavour of its milk, cheese and of course meat, still a traditional Easter dish, once savoured is not easily forgotten and indeed remains prized for the management of a variety of health conditions, most notably the allergy-based conditions of eczema and asthma.

It may also have been the giant boulders that lie scattered along the limestone pavement plain, north-east of Mullaghmore, perhaps the Burren's spiritual hub, that first fired my imagination. This became for us the 'Giant's playground' as we conjured images of these great stone forms being scattered like marbles in a childhood game by a prehistoric race of Goliaths. Little did I realise at the time that their origin was indeed prehistoric and not the whim of a great colossus but rather the debris of a retreating glacier. In fact, glaciation has marked this landscape in fascinating ways, first stripping it of its covering soil and then scratching its surface along the direction of retreat, still easily visible today across the mountain bluffs. These surface marks weathered quickly to become deep furrows separating rectangular slabs of rock, the exotically named clints and grykes of our school geography books. Across this ancient playground, we hop-scotched merrily through that maze of erratics, as the sense of the 'other' began to unfold within.

The connection to the beyond was made all the more vivid by tales of the banshee, the repugnant old hag who inhabited so many of the hearth-told stories we listened to as children. Each old Clare family appeared to have a banshee associated with it, and my grandfather's people, the O'Loughlins from Rockforest, were no exception. Again, it was a great limestone boulder, still standing on the roadside from Rockforest to Skahard in the shadow of Mullaghmore, that provided inspiration and substance to one such story. Over twelve feet in diameter and sliced in two as if by a mighty sword, this was the place, we were told, from which the banshee would venture forth to make her hideous lament on the death of an O'Loughlin clan member.

It was in a school geography class that I first discovered the language of this ancient landscape of stone was revealed and mysterious terms like 'reverse transhumance'. This primeval practice, unique in Europe, is where livestock are brought up into the mountains in winter to graze. The traditional term in the Burren for this practice is 'winterage'. I always imagined the mountain stone acting like a giant storage heater drawing in the warmth of the summer sun and slowly releasing this during the winter months. However, the reality is that a generally milder climate (because of the influence of the nearby North Atlantic drift) and the desire to preserve the lower pastures are the predominant drivers of this practice. The wisdom of this is recognised by anyone who has felt the mildness or seen the new growth in a hazel thicket on such a winterage in early January. This fact was not lost even on farmers as far away as County Meath, from where livestock came annually for winter-conditioning and for whom a piece of Burren winterage was a prized possession.

When you are brought up among wild things it is difficult to exist away from them and thus an extended absence was punctuated out of regular necessity with trips to the west. Some alone, on the bus to Gort, from where the journey to the village of Skahard was dominated by the view of Mullaghmore and the eastern Burren escarpment. Some with family or friends where we re-enacted our childhood game of seeking the first drystone wall on the route west, like a tentacle stretching from, and connecting us to, this place of stone. I sought out this time among the stone hungrily as the constant noise and stimulation of the concrete metropolis seemed to deplete me while the quiet mountains seemed always to nourish and sustain.

The Cheyenne used to say that 'nothing lives long only the earth and the mountains', and the Burren mountains evoke that sense of the primordial to many who visit and live there. Although a dull and lifeless landscape to some, this place of stone has always nurtured and renewed me, whether clothed in the purple of a low evening light or glistening brightly after a

The Burren, Ballyvaughan/Fanore coast
© Karin Funke

rain shower. In a time when our environment is suffering such abuse and disregard, we must stop seeing nature as a commodity to be bought and sold as we please but rather see ourselves as temporary guardians of this precious resource. The Burren is one place where wild nature remains at its most apparent and where we have an opportunity to inspire future generations to value and preserve their natural inheritance.

The Publicans' Outlook

Bernadette and Michael Monks

We came from Dublin to Ballyvaughan in 1982, having bought what used to be Peter O'Loghlen's public house. We were very conscious from the beginning that we had stepped into a house and former business that was greatly respected throughout the region, the business of the late Peter O'Loghlen, who was the Dáil deputy for County Clare, and his late wife, a great business woman in her day.

The premises had been completely vacant for about a year so there was a lot of work to be done and we were very anxious to open as quickly as possible. We stayed in Tigín, out on the coast road, while we worked. We did all the work ourselves and we were able, after six weeks, to open the pub, which we named Monks Pub.

We had a few shocks to begin with. Michael went shopping in Ballyvaughan at 7.30 a.m. on one of our first mornings in the village. Nothing was open so he had to return at a reasonable, non-Dublin time, to get what he wanted. We soon became accustomed to the rhythm of our west of Ireland rural life, where the shops open 'late' in the mornings and stay open quite late at night.

When we opened our pub, our first customer was Packy

Michael O'Connor and Mick Carrucan, Monks Pub, Ballyvaughan, 1997
© Michael Monks

Vaughan. He hailed Michael, 'Ah, the Dublin Jackeen. If any more of you come, I'll take myself off.' Michael O'Connor, Paddy Mullins, Jimmy Burns, Tony Garrihy and Mick Carrucan followed Packy. They were all not just loyal customers but friends. They were also real characters, full of good humour, unimpressed by show-offs.

Music was one of the pub's strengths and it even had its own band called U-4, the members being Steve Moore, John Hogan, Michael Davoren and Mick Carrucan. The fun and laughter of those evenings is still with us.

One evening we will always remember: Michael O'Connor, one of the last riders of the famous 'black bikes' of the west of Ireland, lived in a little house on the coast road, not far from the pub. Each day he polished his brass knocker until it shone to the heavens. Every morning Michael passed, on his bike, on the way to the village to get his newspaper from MacNeill

(O'Loghlen) and his supplies from either Jim Hyland or Mrs Linnane. He always wore a dark suit, charcoal grey or black, sometimes with a very faint pinstripe (a loud pinstripe he'd consider vulgar). Michael had been a tailor in his working days so he kept a very fine crease on his trousers, a crease you 'could sharpen stainless steel knives on'. He sometimes stopped at MacNeill's pub for a glass on his way home.

Every evening faithfully he came to our pub, but he always had to rush away so that he could see the daily episode of his favourite television programme, *Coronation Street*. One day an actor from the programme came into the pub and Michael (Monks) introduced Michael O'Connor as a fan and the two sat together chatting away. She bought her fan a brandy and a photo was taken of the pair and it was in the *Clare Champion*, the local newspaper. This was one of Michael O'Connor's greatest days.

Michael regularly asked Michael (Monks), 'Michael, will you drive me down to Nagels in Kilfenora. I want to buy a new suit.' Of course it was always Nagels where Michael bought his clothes, he would never dream of going anywhere else. Sometimes if the suit didn't quite fit he would say, 'That's all right – I'll fix it myself.' And so he would, with his skill as a former tailor standing to him.

Once in the 1980s, Murphy's Stout decided to raffle a colour television set in our pub in order to publicise their stout. All customers who bought a pint of Murphy's stout were given a ticket with their pint. Each ticket had to be filled in with the customer's name and address and the raffle was to take place after a month. Michael O'Connor decided to drink a few pints, hoping to be lucky. He really wanted to win so that he could watch *Coronation Street* in colour – he only had a black and white television. On the night of the raffle, a big crowd gathered in the pub. Beforehand we made two identical boxes: one was filled with tickets all with Michael's name and the other contained the tickets with all the other names. To make everything look above board we asked the parish priest to draw the winning ticket. There was nearly universal surprise and delight when Michael's name was announced as the winner of the colour television. We very speedily disposed of the box containing all the tickets with Michael's name on them and just as quickly we produced for examination the second box – there were a few characters who were suspicious. They checked this box carefully and found all to be fair and square. Michael was walking on air as now he could watch his favourite programme in colour. His photo was taken at the presentation and he appeared in the *Clare Champion*. Michael never knew of our fixing the draw and he lived for many years to enjoy *Coronation Street*.

Another regular customer was Tony Gerrihy. People will remember Tony as the man with the donkey and cart and

Michael Monks and Michael O'Connor with the winning ticket for the colour TV, Monks Pub, Ballyvaughan, 1997 © Michael Monks

the little dog who always parked in the centre of the village under the signposts. We gave Tony his midday meal and kept a friendly eye on him to make sure he did not drink too much.

Once Tony was to go to America to see his sister. I offered to drive him to Shannon airport and went over to Tony's early to see if he was ready and sober. He'd done no packing at all so I went home to get him a suitcase. I put a few things in and we set off for the airport. He made me stop in Corofin, where he bought four pounds of sausages, pounds and pounds of rashers, black pudding and even more of white pudding. I stayed on in Shannon for a while because I was nervous about whether he'd take the flight. I explained the situation to one of the gardaí on duty and asked if I could go in and make sure he got on the plane. He gave me permission and I discovered Tony had boarded the plane. A month later I met him at Shannon airport. He arrived not just with one suitcase but with several, all full of new suits. He also had a new watch and $1,000. He was wearing a new suit and in the lapel of the jacket was a red rose!

Tony Gerrihy with his donkey and dog

Settling In to the Right Place

Sarah Poyntz

We (Mary Ann, a friend, and I) did a tour of the west of
Ireland in the 1970s and we came upon a very small village
with thatched rental cottages. We thought it very beautiful.
Almost a decade later, when we wished to holiday in Ireland
again, we remembered this village. We decided to rent one of
the cottages and I wrote to Shannon Tourism for a brochure.
We'd forgotten the name of the village but on examining the
information booklet, we found our holiday cottage. When we
arrived in Ballyvaughan in 1983, to our surprise we realised we
had *never* seen it before.

We decided to retire to Ballyvaughan because we took to
the people, grew to love the Burren and were pleased with the
facilities we found in the village in the 1980s. We were the
'blow-ins', Mary Ann from the States and I from the great
model county, Wexford.

The two people we first came across were Maura Mooney-
Hynes and Seán MacNeill O'Loghlen. Maura, who ran the post
office, then on Main Street, put herself out to help us, telling
us where to buy briquettes for the fire in the cottage; where we
could fill up our petrol tank; how to use the telephone nearby

– an antique instrument, so antique that it made us nervous. You entered the telephone booth, picked up the phone and then cranked away with a handle until the voice at the other end answered. Then you asked for the number you wished to contact. Various clinks, clunks and clanks were heard, and finally you were through. There wasn't really much delay and it was all very human – you could always say a word to Maura if she was not busy. The post office is now in Ballyvaughan Service Station, where it is run by Maura's daughter-in-law, Siobhain. Maura was a source of wonder to me – she was so quick with the sums compared to myself. This ability, together with the facility of remembering, is a characteristic of the local people – no need for computers to remind them. They forestalled all those 'techie' things.

Both Maura and Seán MacNeill O'Loghlen told us about Claire's Restaurant. We spent many, many evenings eating Claire's delicious dinners and listening to Manus (Walsh) play the piano. We took all our friends there, from the States, France, Britain, and we were never disappointed. The restaurant had style, the food and service were impeccable and the prices were good. It was the friendliest place, where good cheer and genuine hospitality were of the greatest importance.

Our other initiator into the life of the village was Seán MacNeill O'Loghlen, farmer, Whiskey Pub owner and the supervisor of 'Rent an Irish Cottage'. When we entered the darkish pub to announce our arrival and collect our key, we beheld a fine-looking man wearing a dark suit, white shirt and dark tie. We looked at him and much more important *he* looked at us, assessing us in his inimitable way, giving us that long, appraising regard as he wondered, 'How am I going to manage these rental people?' And manage us he did until the day he died.

Nothing escaped MacNeill. He never suffered fools gladly and he always referred to us as 'the ladies'. He told us that people came from many countries to rent the cottages, from Britain, France, America, Germany, etc., and that if the rented cottage accommodated five people then these people came with five or less but if Irish people rented a cottage for five then they came with eight, nine, ten, and then they were 'all over the place, on top of each other'.

Also in the village itself was Hyland's Hotel. Here too the food was excellent, and Marie, Deirdre and Jim always made us welcome with our guests. There were two grocery shops, one run by Jim (Hyland), ably assisted by Madeleine Deeley. Shortly after our arrival, we went into Jim's to shop. Mary Ann asked him where we could buy flowers – her children were about to visit. Jim gave that wonderful smile of his and said, 'The man that would sell flowers in Ballyvaughan would see more dinner-times than dinners.'

Yet another reason we decided to settle in Ballyvaughan for our retirement was Monks Pub, owned by Bernadette and Michael Monks. This pub was unique, the food was top class, the service friendly and the prices affordable. French tourists heard about the pub and came in their legions, passing the word to their compatriots. The Americans flocked to it – the pub hit the food section of the *New York Sunday Times*. We have never eaten better mussels, crab and lobster than those served to us by the Monks family.

Animals are often a good way to meet decent people. When we first retired to Ballyvaughan, we needed someone to look after our little dog, Courgie (Courgette), and our cat, Catlean (a stray from New Ross). Our first carer was the late Betty Boyle, who had a great way with animals. Courgie was very happy with Betty and somewhat reluctant to return home with us.

The late Colm Walsh, our vet, treated Courgie at the end of her life. He sometimes used acupuncture and I will never forget the sight of the tall, handsome man sitting in our living room with the little dog on his knees while he carefully placed needles in her tummy. There was not a whimper from her. Later Colm and Douglas Culligan came to put her down and were very gentle with the little scrap.

On our walks we often stopped to speak with the late Jimmy Burns. He would chat to us about his animals, horses, a donkey and his cattle, and we spoke about our cat and dog. One day we told Jimmy that the cat would be ten in a few days. A glint came into his eyes and he asked, 'Can I tell Michael Monks that you're giving a birthday party for the cat?'

'Of course you can,' we replied.

Next day we met Bernadette.

'Bernadette,' we asked, 'did Jimmy tell Michael we were giving a birthday party for our cat?'

'Yes, he did,' said Bernadette.

'And what did Michael say?'

'Sure, he said "They're half cracked out there!"'

We always gave the late Tom Beg, a fluent Irish speaker, a lift out to his home in Gleninagh. I remember his account of some of his relatives who had emigrated to America. He said they had no English and they couldn't write home because they couldn't address the letters. One day while chatting with him, we mentioned that we loved the rowan tree. 'I'll get you one from the mountain,' he said. Shortly afterwards Tom died when his house went on fire. We went to his mass and on the way home I said, 'We'll never have a rowan tree now.' About five weeks after that we noticed a small tree in what we call our Grove. It was a rowan tree planted for us by Tom Beg – he never told us he'd planted it. It is now about two metres high and always full of berries in the autumn.

I called MacNeill our guru, and we have never had a better one. In 1985, with Mary Ann's two children, Annie and Liam (William), we decided to retire to Ballyvaughan so we set about finding a house. Various estate agents showed us houses: one smelt so much of face powder that the scent would, we thought, never be eliminated; another had been the home of a retired English couple who had been drowned off Doolin Pier and still had all their personal belongings strewn about; others had poor roofs, rising damp and wide cracks in the walls. We were beginning to despair.

Then MacNeill took charge: one morning we went into MacNeill's to buy *The Irish Times* and he said, 'I think I have a site for you. Come back in ten minutes and I'll drive you out to see it. It has full planning permission.' He drove us out the coast road and showed us the site of almost four acres. We tried to walk the site but we lost MacNeill and went about calling, 'MacNeill … MacNeill, where are you?' He then told us that the man who owned the site, P. J. O'Grady of Lisdoonvarna, was working in a field nearer the village and said, 'Don't be haggling with him now. Pay the price the man is asking and let you all sign up there and then. I'll witness it.' We followed all MacNeill's instructions – orders would be a better word – and everything was regulated with the solicitors. We had a site and then P. J., an engineer, and the Shannon Brothers built our house from autumn 1985 to spring 1986. Here we have spent some of the happiest years of our lives and each day as we look at the beautiful, unique Burren, its glorious sea and landscape, we thank MacNeill.

When the house was built and when we still had to be in America – Mary Ann was still teaching at Cornell University – MacNeill looked after the house. He used to go out after his pub was closed for the night and he sat there for about fifteen to thirty minutes. He said he'd read most of the biography of William Butler Yeats' father while there. MacNeill would not hear of being paid a fee for looking after our house.

Later when his wife, May, became very ill we wondered what we could do to help. We decided, after MacNeill told us that she would sleep downstairs in one of the sitting-rooms, that we would buy her a little television set with a remote control that she could use from her bed. We gave it to Peter, their son, and next day MacNeill thanked us and said, 'I have been doing things for people all my life and I've never looked for anything back and seldom got it …' He was very moved.

MacNeill was a great Fianna Fáil man – his father was the TD for Clare. During one election, there was a large box of Fianna Fáil rosettes on the pub counter. At that time, sweets were sold in the bar, and after school a group of young boys, most of whose families belonged to Fine Gael, came in to buy sweets. One of the children, pointing to the colourful rosettes, said, 'They're lovely.' MacNeill presented each of them with a rosette and they all disappeared with them proudly displayed on their chests. He was delighted to see the Fine Gael children run off wearing the Fianna Fáil badges of honour.

He told us about two local brothers who 'could carve anything out of wood. But, you know, I've often noticed that talented people like that always seem to have a flaw and with them it was the drink. They had a cottage out the road there and they'd come home of an evening and have their bit to eat. They'd then pull on a rope hanging from the ceiling over their heads and above the table. This would lower a small bath onto the table. It would be full of the poitín. They'd drink themselves nearly under the table but they never forgot to pull on the rope to get the bath of poitín back up among the rafters. 'Twas illegal of course and they were afraid of the Revenue and guards.'

MacNeill didn't like to see people drunk and had the greatest admiration for the Welsh musicians who come over to Ballyvaughan every year to play in the local pubs. 'They come into the pub here at about 11 a.m. and they stay for hours and hours and you'd see each of them with the one pint for a very long time and no boasting about them or betting to see who'd drink the most.'

He never failed to check up on us – one time I got a fish bone stuck in my gum between two teeth and phoned MacNeill to ask for the dentist's (Leonard Culligan) phone number. While my friend Mary Ann was on the phone, I managed to get the bone out so I did not need to go and next day MacNeill asked, 'Why didn't you phone Leonard? He was up waiting for you, all dressed up in his white coat.'

Another time Mary Ann was awakened by a voice saying, 'Hello, you there, will you give me a lift?'

She saw a large white face looking in at her through her opened bedroom window. She dashed down the corridor into my bedroom and woke me up saying, 'There's a man outside wanting a lift.'

I stuck my head out through my window to find a man drunk there, 'Will yous gimme a lift?' he asked.

'Indeed we won't,' I replied, 'you get off home with you now and don't be bothering us. Off you go and I'm phoning the guards this minute.'

Neither of us knew who he was. I did phone the guards and

two delightful, handsome gardaí came over from Ennistymon and went all over the property with their flashlights – not a sign of anyone. Next day MacNeill said before we could utter a word, 'I hear you had the guards out there last night.'

When we told him our story he said, 'Any trouble you have like that you only have to phone us and we'll be out.'

We relied on MacNeill and if you had a friend in Seán MacNeill O'Loghlen, you had a friend for life. He was the most loyal of men, the truest of human beings.

The Ladies' Club

The Ladies Club largely dominated the second half of the 1980s in Ballyvaughan. It got things done, and thanks to them, the old national school was renovated to become St John's Village Hall. They raised money until they had the entire cost, which was well over IR£40,000, through sales of work, raffles, get-togethers and donations. The energy expended was astounding because the village had a population of only 400 souls.

On one beautiful summer day, the ladies took a very short break from their activities and went for a banana boat trip in Ballyvaughan Bay (on an inflatable boat shaped like a banana towed by a motor-boat). Some of the ladies swung their legs elegantly over the boat and held on. They set off cheered by the cowards left behind. The motor-boat surged out into the bay and then circled at speed. Naturally the banana boat's passengers were flung off into the vast and mightily deep waters – intentionally of course. Maura Mullins, who could not swim, sank but rose again and found herself surrounded by strange creatures. She shouted out a warning, 'Shark!' The sharks were very friendly, even prepared to nuzzle up to the ladies, who by this time were 'vaulting' back onto the banana boat. The sharks turned out to be dolphins.

About this time there was a plan for a fin fish farm quite near Ballyvaughan. This of course was (and is) a famous shellfish area. It never succeeded because the people of the village, endowed with common sense, would have none of it. The campaign against it was a great success. As was another splendid campaign at about the same time, the campaign against the proposed visitor centre at lovely Mullaghmore, one of the glories of the Burren. This became a national campaign against the official policy of the government of the time. Once again, the people won and we could not help but admire one of the most likeable characteristics of the Ballyvaughan people – they were not afraid to speak their minds and to act in accordance.

Gleninagh, the First Blow-ins

Pat Browne

In 1919 Canon James Jackson Griffin was appointed rector of Ennis and lived in Bindon Street with his wife, Evelyn, and their seven children (Charles, Cyril, Primrose, Robin, Muriel, Gerald and Frank). The three eldest boys were at school with Samuel Beckett at Portora Royal School, Enniskillen, County Fermanagh. Evelyn, an intrepid early driver, frequently took the family to Kilkee and later to the North Clare coast, the Flaggy Shore. From there, they visited Gleninagh, and the canon, a fun-loving man, loved to chat with the local people, especially with Stephen Hynes. The family loved Gleninagh, especially the views across the bay to the Martello tower at Finavarra and further to the Galway coast. They rented the O'Donoghue Cottage (now Scheunemanns') from Clare County Council for holidays. Later the canon persuaded Stephen to sell him half an acre of land by Gleninagh Pier.

In 1942, the land was registered to the canon and plans were drawn up on the lines of a council house but with some modifications, one being high ceilings. No one ever knew the reason for this and it was a cause of continual wonder since none of the family was tall. Jack Doherty of Fanore was the

Currach at Gleninagh Pier, 1970s
© Pat Browne

builder and the construction was financed by the canon and by Primrose's husband, Bill Browne. They received a loan from Clare County Council of £199 13s 5d. There was no mains water or electricity, and rainwater was collected in drums from the downpipes or in buckets from the mountain stream by the Burns' house (now the entrance to the old road opposite the beginning of the road to the pier).

During the Emergency it was very difficult to get construction materials. The slates were second-hand from Galway Jail (now the cathedral site) and the window frames and shutters were from the demolished Coole Park House (the former home of Lady Gregory). Conditions were primitive and there were young grandchildren coming from far-flung places (India, Nigeria) with their parents for holidays so it was decided to add a kitchen with a large water tank, together with an outside chemical toilet.

Evelyn died in 1943 and the canon moved to Glengarrif,

Gleninagh Pier, 2009
© Karin Funke

County Cork, in 1947 and became much less involved in the running of the cottage, especially after he remarried. He gave the cottage to Charles in 1950 and from then on Charles and his siblings shared the responsibility for it. They all contributed financially to the upkeep and to improvements like a cement patio, an additional water tank over the new turf house, gas lighting and a new cement roof. Another of the canon's sons, Gerald, on becoming the first manager of Aillwee Cave, lived for a time at the cottage and later bought a property at Abbey Hill, New Quay. The cottage became a holiday home for my mother, father and siblings during the month of August every year, while my uncle Frank and his wife, Sue, came in July. These two families became tenants in common.

In the 1960s, the Brownes became the principal users of the cottage and I became the most regular of the inhabitants. Primrose, my mother, wouldn't hear of changing anything.

She seemed to love and thrive on the discomfort – she was always ready to describe how she survived the winter of 1947 (a fiercely cold winter with long periods of snow and black ice). She swam in the sea off Gleninagh every morning until well into her eighties. All guests were welcome, German, Italian, long lost relatives, even if they had to pitch their tents in the garden. The biggest event was in 1990 when sixty relations descended on Gleninagh and Ballyvaughan to celebrate my parents' golden wedding anniversary. Lunch was in Gleninagh and dinner at Hyland's Hotel. The cottage saw the last visits of my father, Bill, and my mother, Primrose, in the late 1990s.

The cottage had become very dilapidated. Brownes and Griffins consulted with Frank Stafford of Axis Architects and had the cottage re-developed by John Connole from 2004 to 2005. Guests and owners attest to its success. The story of the cottage is also the story of the family who lived there, finding peace and quiet just as my family still do.

THE ROLE OF THE BLOW-IN
Mary Ann Nevins Radzinowicz

The role of the blow-in is to fit in and muck in, and the major impediment to that is self-consciousness. The blow-in gardener, for example, feels herself in a compromised position. Out of respect for the Burren, she will not plant a loud imported purple prunus and she will watch out for the dreaded interloper, the Japanese knotweed. As a blow-in, though, she asks herself, 'Am I not both the loud purple prunus and the Japanese knotweed?'

Fitting in is not achieved by the non-Irish blow-in by trying to look, sound or feel Irish. He or she will never learn to spell correctly any Irish word, including political titles, proper names, or polite toasts in pubs, and their cúpla focal will seem well-spoken only to the kindliest of their teachers. If Irish blow-ins feel like outsiders on any of these accounts, they at least know better what they are outside of.

Fitting in doesn't come easier with time but the blow-in needs to join in: if he can, he joins the church, and if he is not a church-goer, he takes bridge lessons and joins a bridge club. The membership of both church and bridge club overlaps considerably, from high to low or clerical to lay. Immediately he or she is in the loop and will not be the last to hear any news good, bad, or churchyard conjectural.

St John's Hall has witnessed the usefulness of the blow-in: those who baked cakes and foreign-tasting cookies for sale at the Christmas party or who made things for the Farmers' Market and who bought those goods. Blow-in usefulness extends to daily picking up stuff people have thrown on the pavements and seasonally cleaning up Bishop's Quarter beach. The rock-solid basis on which the blow-in stands is their contribution to the economy. All blow-ins pay tax and few become charges to the community. Sometimes a blow-in will open a cave or build a seafood restaurant or found a magazine or run rent-a-cottages and will give employment both to natives and non-natives; quite often natives of Ballyvaughan will open a shop or a garage or a garden maintenance where blow-ins work and help out.

A blow-in's sense of non-belonging is largely self-generated, then. If that is not exactly the blow-in's impression, there is only one further role to play. The corollary to fit in and muck in, is don't give out.

COULD I REALLY LIVE HERE?
Fiona Monks

I will always remember my first morning walking the craig (stony ground) down to the shoreline, and wondering as a child of seven does, where did all the rock come from? I was intrigued by the alien landscape as I stepped and stumbled and gaped to see what was between the crevices of the many funny-shaped stones. Could I really live here? But gradually I began to settle into life in the Burren, and a very special person, Jimmy Burns, helped this along. Jimmy was a great horseman and through our mutual love of horses our friendship was firmly cemented. He taught me to appreciate the landscape as we rode on horseback over the hills, along bóithríns, and each year we would compete to see who would be the first person to hear the cuckoo. He was so in tune with life in the Burren and its surroundings that on a spring morning we could cheat the high tide, cross the channel at the Weathercock and gallop from Monks Pub across the bay to Bishop's Quarter and back before we were caught in the rising, incoming tide. They were

Jimmy Burns (left)
© Michael Monks

magical times as we felt we owned the world, with nothing disturbing our thoughts but the sound of hoof-beats ringing in our ears. Jimmy allowed me to befriend this once alien place, and when I walk the winding road up Gleninagh Mountain, I place a pebble on the mass rock he showed me and I say a special 'thank you' to him for enriching my life.

A Burren Story
Ann O'Connor & Brendan Dunford

Ann O'Connor:

I first came to the Burren on holiday as a fifteen-year-old and stayed with a German husband and wife whose daughter Eva was my 'very best friend'. Coming from a family of nine children, I certainly enjoyed the comfort and novelty of staying with Eva's delightfully small family at the holiday cottages in Ballyvaughan. The Freidrichs were enthralled by the west of Ireland and particularly the Burren. I was a nosey and curious child and I loved discovering things. So the Burren was a natural Eden for me.

The Germans actually educated me to the wonders of the place. 'Ze geology and historical wealth of ze Burren', Werner would insist, was seriously under threat by neglect. 'Ve need to doo something,' he would declare over breakfast. I was not sure how kindly I took to Werner's depictions of the need for European control on what I would have considered (at the time) entirely an Irish matter. I was merely a schoolgirl with no resources to fund great plans for saving the world, but nonetheless I listened attentively, heeding Werner's wise words. That time in the Burren I was wide awake to learning and energised with possibilities. The landscape of the Burren quickly filled my imagination with stories of the past, led me to dream wildly of the future and teased me with new promise.

Over the next few years, I finished school and dragged myself through college with very little idea of what I wanted to do. I always thought I would head west, maybe to County Kerry, home of my forebears. But like many others, life was dictated by the dismal economy of the late 1980s. We all travelled in droves east towards Holyhead. For a while, I felt a little lost in London and immersed myself completely in my work. My time followed a hectic pattern for many years, day after day, one business meeting after another, sandwiched between the demands of my domestic life. By the early 1990s I was a single mother who ran a small technology company. As far as I was concerned, the life I had once imagined as a fifteen-year-old had not even started to reveal itself.

In many ways my daughter Caoimhe and I were lucky; London offered us a somewhat secure future. We had good friends; materially we had all we needed, including a nice apartment and a good income. But it didn't feel like home. In the late 1990s, I made fresh plans and returned to Ireland. For a year I commuted back and forth to London until one day I could do it no more. It was during this year and a chance visit to Clare in 1998, that my life detoured – actually, I changed maps altogether. Encouraged by my brother to 'live a little' I headed west to Miltown Malbay. It was early July and 'Willie Week' was in full swing. The impact of that random visit still reverberates for me today: I fell in love with the man of my dreams.

Brendan Dunford:
Though I'd passed through a few times, my first real visit to the Burren was in 1997, as a student from University College

Dublin. I'd just finished a course there in Environmental Resource Management and was offered a research position to find out more about the impact of farming on the heritage of the Burren. I immediately liked that the research was about people, and not just an abstract piece of work. Though I knew a little about farming, having grown up on a farm in County Waterford, I knew nothing about the Burren other than what I'd read in books, so I felt that I would have to move there if I was to do any sort of justice to the subject.

The Teagasc Walsh Fellowship Scheme funded my study, so I was quite lucky. Still, living on £100 a week for the four years that followed demanded certain sacrifices and no small amount of luck. The latter came my way in the form of NUI Galway who, for a modest rent, allowed me to stay in their field study centres in Carron (six months) and Finavarra (almost three years!). I loved the Flaggy Shore, it was my first real home from home and offered a beautiful, isolated, albeit frugal, existence which really cemented my relationship with the Burren and its natural wonders.

Transport was a bigger problem. I started with a push-bike. I was a lot fitter then and remember cycling regularly from Carron to Ennis for meetings, still breathless as I sat around the table with my suited supervisors. Soon I graduated to a motorbike, a beat-up Yamaha 125, a cursed machine which kept breaking down, always at the wrong time. But I guess it got me around, and certainly got me known – a 6ft 3ins man straddling such a machine on the winding roads of the Burren did leave an abiding image among many who still remember the bike that I've long since tried to forget.

I loved the Burren from the day I started here. There was so much to see and learn, so much colour, so much mystery, so much to explore. Getting around on the bike meant that I could get to places that cars and buses couldn't and see places that most people didn't. Tim Robinson's map was a constant companion. After a while, I started getting to know people, at mass, at the pub, or just out. I'd imagine most people thought I was just another annoying student who would be gone before too long; I myself had no such plans, either to stay or to leave. Like most things in my life, the place just happened to grow on me and I grew into it.

The study was very tough to begin with: I really had no idea what I was supposed to be doing or how, and there wasn't very much support at that time, particularly as I was a long way removed from the college. Most of the data I collected in the first year of work had to be discarded as I realised how many mistakes I'd made. At times, I was despondent. But I persisted – when you put so much time and effort into something it's hard to give up, and as time passed I gradually gained a little more confidence.

I always enjoyed socialising, I love music and the odd pint. I was a bit stranded in Finavarra, not much money and poor transport, but the odd session in Linnanes kept me sane. Occasionally I made a longer foray, and one of my favourite outings was – and still is – to Miltown Malbay in July for Willie Clancy week. It was there, back in 1998, that I met Ann O'Connor, in the pub called Clearys, or 'the Blondes'. Though neither of us realised it at the time, life would never be the same again!

After our meeting in Miltown, we started 'seeing' each other – no easy feat when we lived and worked on opposite sides of the country. It's funny how fast things happen though: within two years we were all living in Finavarra and our gorgeous new baby Alannah was scrambling along the limestone slabs of the Flaggy Shore! Though we only spent a year there and though it wasn't exactly the lap of luxury, it was a very special time: the walks along the shore, the big open driftwood fire, and the rickety ladder up to the attic where months of self-imposed solitary confinement were spent in writing up the PhD.

Within another year, we had moved to a new house near Kinvara. The study had been published as *Farming and the Burren* and later went on to form the basis for the Burren LIFE project or Burrenbeo (an organisation promoting farming in the Burren and protecting the Burren's environment), which continues today with a superb, dedicated team of people in Carron. Back at home the family was growing, with our son Senan born in 2004 (at our house in Kinvara) and Osgar born in 2006. But another birth of sorts had preceded these welcome arrivals: in 2002, while walking in the Burren, we conceived the idea of Burrenbeo – the living Burren.

The idea behind Burrenbeo was that we would combine our skills to bring the story of the Burren to life, initially as a website, www.burrenbeo.com. It was a painstaking exercise, taking months of work – in the end it took nearly five hours to upload the first version of the website using our landline, and we had astronomical phone bills. When we did launch it back in 2002 though, it was one of the best nights of our lives. The Burren College of Art was packed, everybody was so positive, and the initiative was acclaimed in national papers and on television. Burrenbeo, our fifth and most troublesome child, was well and truly born and baptised!

Since then Burrenbeo has gone from strength to strength and we are immensely proud of it. The website has over three million hits annually and is still run on a voluntary basis, though we did receive support to enhance it in later years. We opened a little shop and café in Kinvara to provide information about the Burren and designed a schools' education programme – Eco Beo – from which over 500 young Burren people have so far graduated as 'Burren experts'. We produced a CD-ROM and some interactive games for kids to learn about the Burren, and to encourage them to be proud and protective of their home and their heritage.

But, as with all children, eventually you have to let them go. In 2008, Burrenbeo grew up, went out into the big bad world and became the Burrenbeo Trust, a registered charity. It is now a fully fledged membership-based organisation with a separate board of directors and patrons including people like Seamus Heaney, Bishop Willie Walsh and Professor David Bellamy. We are both deeply humbled by its success and confident of its future as an independent advocate for the Burren.

As we write, all of our children are in school, and we're happily living in Kinvara. Burren LIFE or Burrenbeo is coming to the successful conclusion of its pilot phase and is looking forward to bigger and better things. The Burrenbeo Trust has its first employee, a growing membership and is remaining true to its ideals. Looking to the future, we see great times ahead for the Burren but great challenges too. For us the Burren is a place whose time is yet to come. We have mixed feelings about this because we love that the Burren is still so undiscovered, but we also think there is a need to come up with ways of keeping the communities of the Burren alive, keeping schools and services open, and to do that we need to be more creative in managing the place and using it to deliver new opportunities and a bright future. We're thrilled to be part of the story of the Burren in some small way, and we look forward to more adventures in this special place that we are truly, deeply blessed to call home.

Thank you, Whitethroats
Emma Stewart Liberty

'It's the Burren this year.'

'The where?'

'The Burren – it's in County Clare. We're counting whitethroats.'

'Not Donegal then?' When opportunities arose, all our previous visits had been home to Donegal and it was hard to hide my disappointment when, in January 1985, my aunt rang me from England to tell me where she was doing that year's bird census.

Nevertheless, Paul and I set off from Dublin very early one beautiful Sunday morning that May. The journey took a lot longer then we expected, so our first amazing view of the Burren hills was particularly welcome after nearly five hours in a beat-up Renault 4. We had never seen anything like it and neither of us could believe the scenery at first – the shapes of the terraced hills, the limestone pavements, as we learned to call them, the hawthorn bushes smothered in their whipped-cream blossom, the beautiful ruins of ancient churches. One thing we did know – we had arrived somewhere very special.

During that gloriously warm and sunny week we saw everything that the Burren is famous for in May: gentians, orchids, mountain avens, fairy foxgloves and in addition, dolphins, great northern divers, choughs, as well as whitethroats, the latter being the reason for our presence.

We were hooked. From then on we were back in Bally-vaughan at every possible opportunity, weekends, holidays, birthday treats – any time we could manage to get away we headed straight for Clare. The magic has never disappeared for us, not even after the coldest, wettest, most miserable Easter weekend ever. Still the treasures were there to be looked for, not always found, but the joy even greater when they were – the maidenhair fern, the dark hellebore, my first ever fly orchid, with Mullaghmore as a background – could it get any better?

Dreams were dreamt, plans hatched and money saved, and so it is that for the last ten years Ballyvaughan has been our home place and we can hardly believe it. The initial amazement is only slightly tempered, if at all, by being immersed in a landscape that still inspires and surprises on a daily basis. There is huge pleasure in absorbing the detail that comes with being in a place full-time, the small creeping seasonal changes pinpointing the exact dates of the Brent geese's departure, the sandmartins' arrival, the first cuckoo call and that unmistakable electric blue of the first gentian. We watch the changes on a daily basis because, while we were always weekend walkers, now we walk twice a day because of our involvement with the Irish Guide Dogs. Originally puppy-walkers while we still lived in Dublin, we are now blessed with having Juno and Anna, two of their breeding dogs, living with us full time. Every year we welcome a litter of Retriever or Retriever/Labrador cross puppies. It is the most wonderful thing to be a part of and, while hearts are broken when we have to say goodbye to them after six to seven quick weeks, hearing of their progress (see note on the stages of dog training overleaf) and knowing that they will go on to be helpful companions to people who will love them as much as we do, softens the blow of their departure. Then Paul and

Eleven pups reared by Emma Stewart Liberty and Paul Wojcik
© Emma Stewart Liberty

I can go back to walking their mums and the rest of our dogs in this beautiful place that we have been so fortunate to find and call home. I believe that not all people are lucky enough to find their special place, to be able to say every day, 'Isn't it beautiful?', as we do when looking out over Galway Bay from Bishop's Quarter beach every early morning, no matter what the weather. So it is not surprising that every spring I wait to hear the whitethroats sing and to say a heartfelt 'thank you' to them in return.

The stages of guide dog training

First Stage: from the age of six weeks the guide dog pup lives with a puppy-walker who trains it in acceptable behaviour.

Second Stage: at the age of ten to twelve months the pup goes to a trainer for obedience lessons. The guide dog harness and busy town conditions are introduced. Commands are taught and kerb work, obstacle avoidance, control of distractions. Bus and train travel commence. This takes about two to three months.

Third Stage: the guide dog mobility instructor gives advanced training, developing the dog's skills. This stage also takes from two to three months.

Fourth Stage: the matching of guide dog to owner. This involves a two to three week residential course for both.

Fifth Stage: this is the after-care period, when the guide dog and the owner are visited in the home and any problem is solved.

NOTE: The above procedure is also followed for children with autism, with minor differences.

PARADISE
Jenny Morton

I live in paradise! Where better to live and raise children in these times than in the unpolluted environs of Ballyvaughan? I must admit to not being a city person. In a densely populated area, it is very challenging to find a community. Here, in Ballyvaughan, it is challenging to avoid it!

Our children are like organic chickens and have access to nature's gifts every day of their lives. The older residents of this community, who can trace their ancestry back many years, consistently reminisce on the lost tradition of the meitheal, whereby everyone looked out for and came to the assistance of each other, whether it was turf-cutting, corn-threshing or the slaughtering and preparation of the pig. When I think of life as it is today for the many mothers in this village, I realise that a healthy equivalent to the meitheal still survives. Apart from the safe, clean environment, the community spirit keeps me and my young family here. I do not live in anyone's ear nor does anyone live in mine, but we watch out for one another, especially, as is often the case, when some of our husbands are away earning the daily bread. Some fathers are fortunate to make a living in and around the area but many have to travel to sustain their families. While the cat's away, we mice play in groups to support each other. I know now why I did not thrive in a big city. I hardly ever met my next-door neighbour. If you like connecting with others, this lack of human contact can be a nightmare.

'Cities and towns are so much more convenient,' I hear frequently. But now there are fewer reasons to go miles in the car to sterile supermarkets in search of sustenance for the family because of the revival of the farmers' markets and the trend of growing as much as possible in family gardens. I can see a future when each family will aim to become almost self-sufficient. So perhaps the new traditions will match the old meitheal.

One thing that seems very different today is the proportion of people living here who were born elsewhere. Overall this village shows the way people with different backgrounds can come together, can co-exist in peace and tolerance.

The Musings of Visitors to the Villages
Sue & John Leonard

Our arrival at Ballyvaughan in the summer of 1982 came about as a result of a confusion in bookings by our travel agent. The holiday to the Burren had been suggested by Dick (Sue's father), who knew of the Burren and of my interest in natural history, in particular wild flowers. An eleventh-hour phone call, full of apologies, informed us that the Irish cottage at Kinvara had been double booked and that the only alternative was at Ballyvaughan. As each was unknown to us and one Irish cottage *must* be the same as the next we accepted the change. The comparison between the two was never made as Ballyvaughan has consumed our lives for the ensuing twenty-six years.

O'Loghlen's Whiskey Pub, Ballyvaughan
© *Karin Funke*

MacNeill O'Loghlen, the agent for the Ballyvaughan Irish cottages, was tracked down at one of the bars in the village. There was an instant mutual liking between us. We knew from that moment that the travel agent's error had been to our distinct advantage and all four of us moved into the cottage: Dick and Molly (Susie's parents), and ourselves.

The evening meal was organised for us at Hyland's Hotel by MacNeill and as a result our second friendship in the village was founded – with Michael Greene and his mother, Marie. The standard of food served to us at Hyland's Hotel has rarely been equalled.

On the first night, the moving of a bed on the upper floor of the cottage disturbed our sleep. Investigation found the roof to be leaking over the bed and Dick and Molly were furniture-moving to avoid the drips. We resolved to mention it (not complain) to our new friend, MacNeill.

'It won't happen again,' we were assured, 'because it has rained.'

Apparently the thatched roof had been affected by a prolonged period of dry weather – the thatch 'swells' after rain, so making the roof waterproof. The explanation proved correct, and the movement of furniture was not necessary again during our stay.

Heating the cottage, however, did prove difficult. Commercially produced turf packs were available but kindling wood was non-existent. During our diligent search the following day, it was soon brought home to us how General Ludlow, one of Cromwell's officers, on arriving in the Burren, had said, 'Nor wood enough to hang a man.'

The early evening drinks at O'Loghlen's Bar were accompanied by an avalanche of detail from MacNeill about the Burren and its historic past. Visits to various sites were suggested, enabling us to search out hidden treasures in the wilderness of the Burren about which we would have remained very ignorant had we been left to our own devices. Old churches, derelict villages and relief roads built in the time of the Famine, cooking sites – fulachtaí fia – the turloughs, the wedge tombs, dolmens and shebeens: all there for discovery. Pure, unadulterated magic. One can only wonder what life was like in those far-off times. Imagine illicit drinking in the isolated shebeen on the mountain. No taxi home!

I made my first botanical find before we had even arrived in Ballyvaughan. Stopping on the Corkscrew Hill to admire the view over Ballyvaughan Bay, mountain avens *(Dryas octopela)* immediately caught my attention. Delight overcame me and I was stunned, upon entering the Burren region, by the limestone outcrops, clints and grykes and erratics. Here were the details of a typical karst landscape to delight a geographer like myself. My fellow passengers wondered at my outbursts as one feature was followed by another. Stops were frequent. Fortunately in those early 1980s, vehicles were few and far between and no accidents occurred. Corkscrew Hill was a mecca for orchids. Our searches revealed many species.

Over the years there have been some extraordinary occurrences during our wanderings in the region. One sunny spring morning we decided that a walk on Cappanawalla Mountain might enable us to track down the great butterwort (*Pinguicula grandiflora),* a beautiful insectivorous blue flower which is found in County Kerry and more rarely in Clare. Dick, who accompanied Sue and myself, didn't really know what we were looking for and a call interrupted our search, 'Is this what you're looking for?' There was no sign of the source of the voice but a climb into the surrounding hazel scrub produced what we were hoping to find. There, in all its glory, a stand of great butterwort perched on a wet flush on the limestone. On a subsequent visit to the same Cappanawalla site some years later we found a single white butterwort growing amidst its blue neighbours. We realised this was something special and were shortly joined by Dr Charles Nelson, an authority on the flora of the Burren, who shared our enjoyment.

On another occasion, we sought the Irish orchid *(Neotinea maculata).* Once again, as we tramped the wet grass on the slopes of Black Head, Dick came up trumps. He had a knack of finding treasures for us, always claiming his success could be explained by the fact that he was a Kerryman!

On yet another occasion, during a walk by the sea, a great commotion attracted our attention. About fifty metres above the sea-worn limestone soaring high, a greater black-back gull flapped vigorously, squawking loudly, with a spider crab hanging from one of its legs. After what seemed a long time, the contest ended and the crab came crashing down onto the rocks. Not to be outdone, the black-back swooped down and again picked up the now senseless crab. The gull, soaring high, once more dropped the crab onto the rocks. By this time, the crab had no fight left and the bird soon consumed the soft fleshy parts.

The villages written about in this book all have their own character. Sometimes our visits coincide with election time and placards and posters decorate every available site, especially the telegraph poles and lamp posts. The requirement to remove all traces of canvassing soon after the election results in a dramatic landscape change overnight.

Further insight into the heart of Ballyvaughan is shown in the offering of a mass when Dick died. Our visit to Ireland on that occasion was to return Dick to his beloved Kerry, where we placed his ashes in the Harold family tomb, near Castleisland. We then made our way to Ballyvaughan to visit friends. On arrival we were told that on the following evening a mass would be said in memory of Dick who, apart from twice yearly visits to Ballyvaughan, had no connections with the village.

Ballyvaughan and its environs have changed much over the years. More new houses and cottages dot the landscape. In my opinion the move towards conservation has come too late. In the early 1980s the Burren was untouched and it seemed to me that this treasure needed to remain unchanged. Wild flowers prefer their natural habitat and do not react favourably to supplements. Poulsallagh, once a haven for many wild flowers and plants, is now a target for many thousands of tourists who pour out of their coaches and cars to traipse over the limestone pavements. In due course erosion takes place and the appearance of the landscape changes.

How did you end up here in Ballyvaughan?
Manus Walsh

The question most people ask me is, 'Having been born and brought up in Dublin how did you end up here in Bally-vaughan?'

Well, it all started in the unlikely setting of a holiday fair in the Mansion House in Dublin in 1975. It was there, whilst demonstrating the craft of enamelling (I had taught myself that craft to supplement my painting career) that I met the directors of the castles' branch of Shannon Development and they offered me a position as a working craftsman and artist in the top storey of Dunguaire Castle, Kinvara. There I was to

Manus Walsh in his studio in Ballyvaughan
© Beth O'Connell

work for that summer during the daytime tourist hours and sell my enamel work and paintings.

That hot summer of 1975 was to be my first experience of the Burren. I found a very basic house to rent on the Flaggy Shore in New Quay and the rest of the family followed me down, Claire and the three kids, Ciara, Nadine and Cormac, all very young at the time. I must say it is lovely they are still living here in the Burren and perhaps Neil, the only one of our children born here, will do the same.

We lived in New Quay for about three months. When I cycled through the Burren into Kinvara each day I had no inkling that I would spend the next thirty-three years in Ballyvaughan! Perhaps the Burren, its hills, the sea beside us, were already seeping into my subconscious during that idyllic summer on the Flaggy Shore.

During my time in Dunguaire and my discussions with Shannon Development, our lives changed, and we moved to Ballyvaughan the following year, 1976. The idea at that time was to encourage craftspeople, with the help of some grant aid, to set up craft workshops in villages around County Clare. After much discussion, and with great naivety, we decided to go for this venture, and as Claire had relations in Ballyvaughan, we decided to look for a suitable place there. With the help of Ray Quinn, one of Claire's cousins, we found a house/shop in the centre of the village. After much renovation, it became the Manus Walsh Craftworkshop and, later, Claire's Restaurant.

There were many and varied trials and tribulations over the following years but I always felt and knew that I would stay in the Burren. I knew it was 'my' place.

From the very beginning, the Burren had an influence on both my painting and my craftwork, as it still has. Before coming here in the 1970s I knew nothing of the Burren, but in those early years I used to go for long walks in the hills and by the sea with sketchbook, camera, binoculars, and of course tea and sandwiches. Thus through every season I experienced all the mood changes of this wonderful landscape. Later I took to cycling through the Burren and discovered another way of seeing the countryside. As a painter, I have sought to capture it on canvas and paper: through acrylic, watercolour, collage, oils and whatever medium it takes. Of course it is not an 'easy' landscape. Many people find it foreboding, especially during long and rainy winter days. For some, it can be like living under a wet, grey blanket. Then suddenly the 'pet' days or weeks arrive, changing the mood to make it an inspiring, beautiful place to live in. The Burren is a completely different landscape from any other in Ireland or indeed abroad. This is the challenge for the artist – there are so many changes. It is not always grey: the pink or purple hills in the setting sun; the silver shine of the hills after rain; the gleam of turloughs; the huge moon rising over Moneen – all await discovery for the discerning, the patient. I hope, for whatever years are left to me, to continue my artistic struggle with the Burren.

STONES IN EVERY FERTILE PLACE
Maryangela Keane

In 1534 Connor O'Brien wrote to Charles V outlining how his family came to County Clare. I have decided to do the same, to tell my story of how I came, how I have lived in, learned about and loved the Burren for almost fifty years.

To use the Irish expression, I married into Keane's Hotel in 1962. My husband, Maccon, was the fourth generation to own and manage the hotel, which probably in earlier times had been an inn, situated as it was on the square in Lisdoonvarna. It was a small family-run hotel, nicely furnished and possessing a fine, eclectic library.

After my arrival in May, our first guests were three ladies from Norfolk who arrived by bus. They were all in their seventies, two of them twins who dressed alike. All three were botanists. I appointed myself the task of driving them about to the various sites, so for the following week, armed with packed lunches, we walked the hills and valleys of the Burren. On those walks, they were teaching me and I was learning and listing unfamiliar limestone species.

During my first year, I discovered that our guests were almost exclusively interested in the natural history of the Burren. To facilitate this market we collected a wide-ranging reference library of texts, published papers and maps, and set up small microscopes for more specialised researchers. The guests then were mainly from Great Britain, many of them returning often. Some knew each other, thus creating a house party atmosphere, and we brought together those with similar interests. They were a mixture of amateurs and academics so the evening conversations in the bar were varied and interesting. Gradually, as travel became easier, Dutch, French and Germans arrived. This gave me the opportunity of sitting at the feet of great men, attending nightly lectures in one language or another on some subject or other in my own home!

I have lived many years in this North Clare landscape, the Burren. It means rocky place. Geographically the area has a far wider and more complex sense and meaning. The area stretches around my home like a great horseshoe, its opening to the north-west. The unique appearance bears witness to its boundaries. The Burren lies between the Atlantic coast and a line drawn roughly from Doolin eastward to Corofin and northwards to Gort and Kinvara.

My first encounter with the Burren was a surprise, almost a strange experience. Initially I was startled by the starkness of its grey lunar-like appearance. The bleak stretches of fractured and fretted rock reaching up the hillsides in a seemingly bare, stony, terraced void neither encouraged nor charmed me. The region seemed full of emptiness, space and light. It appeared anchored to this world by endless unyielding rock, hard, harsh, and hostile. I did not, or could not, understand it and with the impatience of ignorance, I dismissed it. Thankfully I was to live to know otherwise, to understand a little more and eventually conduct a secret romance with this classic karst landscape, this strong, secure, sympathetic, supportive stony land.

Later the light impressed. It is clear, radiant, and dazzlingly bright. It can glitter too after a shower when the limestone shines like silver. The understanding of that light is one of the Burren's secrets. The clarity results from the atmosphere being pollution-free. In addition, there is no over-shading shrubbery and little soil to absorb the light that is reflected from the exposed limestone. The light is further enhanced by reflection from the sea. The warm, moist winds originate in the Gulf Stream and are central to this micro-climate. The higher hills have a reverse ground temperature curve, thus promoting the unusual winter growth activity extant today. A combination of environmental circumstances obtains in this land that cannot be duplicated elsewhere. The farmers in the Burren practise transhumance farming – they drive their cattle up the hills in November to avail of this winter grazing until May.

The Burren is a paradox, an enigma. What appears at first to be a bare, petrified desert is a metropolis of natural history. It is a fertile, fragile, plant-rich landscape that has supported people and their animals for thousands of years. During that time, man has altered the landscape with his many constructions indicative of his living, farming, fighting, worshipping, dying, burying. So from the post-glacial period we can read the landscape from the traces of its people as clearly as reading their history from the pages of a book.

Umpteen euphoric terms are used to describe the impact, diversity, strangeness and beauty of the Burren. These descriptions pale into insignificance compared to learning the science of the Burren: the reasons, causes, effects that unite to create the reality of today. In the beginning my interests were quite exclusive, only archaeology or botany. Now, however, I am not so interested in the specifics but in their interdependency and explicit dependency on the limestone. This did not come overnight but as a result of reading, recording, learning, listening and talking. I have been enriched by experts, revisionists in books and conversations.

Winter walking in the Burren is an exceptional and unique experience. The anticipation and expectation of spring and summer has passed, a certain stillness sets in as if nature itself is at rest. It is my belief that the singular magic of a place is evident from what has happened there or from what befalls us when in its vicinity. In this theatre of stone, there are no noises, only sounds of our footsteps on rock, sounds of wind in harmony with sea, the lowing of cattle. This is a place where the past, present, future seem to blend in the timelessness of the rock itself. I suppose, put more simply, the scientific phenomena of the Burren can be explained but the spiritual phenomena have to be experienced:

Of the life to come, what I hear is the murmur
Of underground streams, what I see is a limestone landscape.

W. H. Auden

Reversal Contrary to Expectation
Gordon Teskey

In Greek drama there is often a moment of illumination where
an aspect of a story is suddenly revealed. It was such a sense
of illumination that I experienced at my first sight of the bare,
flat-topped, striated limestone hills of the Burren, in County
Clare. I grew up under a worn-down mountain range, like
aged teeth, where thousands of miles of exposed, Precambrian
rock, much of it granite and gneiss, are covered in forest, cut
up by swift, shallow rivers, and dotted with innumerable lakes.
The water flows and pools wherever it can on an impermeable
surface of stone, forming large lakes at the lower elevations
and, at the higher elevations, beaver-ponds choked with dead
trees. In contrast, the Burren ground is an ancient seabed thrust
up from below, composed of tiny creatures that died and sank
to the bottom, crushed over millennia into innumerable strata.
The dried seabed has been broken by pressure, turned sideways
and thrust up into hills, exposing the layers at crazy angles.
The forests that once grew there were cut down and burned
in prehistory, at the beginning of farming, but tough holly
and thorn bushes have colonised the lower slopes, clustering
among small stands of hazel. The bare hills are criss-crossed
up to their summits with ancient walls made of piled stones
which also date back to prehistory, as do the megalithic tombs
that appear unexpectedly, huge stones placed horizontally
over vertical uprights. The ground is so porous that, after rain,

Stephen Doolin's climín for harvesting the seaweed at Ballyvaughan
© *Karin Funke*

Stephen Doolin, Ballyvaughan
© *Karin Funke*

ephemeral streams and shallow lakes or turloughs disappear into the ground to flow eventually into the sea.

The Burren landscape was for me a reversal contrary to expectation, being thrust up instead of ground down; porous instead of hard, and barren instead of forested. Fires are not made with birch logs and pine but with neat rectangles of turf cut from the ground, the bog. Instead of appearing to be indifferent to the passage of human beings, the Burren is scribbled over with graffiti of human labour and the detritus of human hope. It is also affected by the nearness of the sea. I don't mean just the salt air and the mudflats within reach of the tides, like those at Bell Harbour, or the jutting piers of limestone along the Rine. I mean the cooperative life that the sea enforces on people who live near it for travel, transport and trade, and above all for work, fishing, of course, but also harvesting the huge mats of seaweed blown in by storms. You can still see the old fishing boats, the currachs, at Gleninagh Harbour and sometimes one of the black-hulled Galway hookers passing that plied these coasts in the age of sail, 'tough trees for masts / rooted in salt water', as the poet Moya Cannon describes them in 'Turf Boats'.

Ballyvaughan sits below Lisdoonvarna on Ballyvaughan Bay, which is a loop in the larger Galway Bay, across which the lights of Galway can be seen at night. In the nineteenth century, the hot springs at Lisdoonvarna drew tourists who came in by sea and were taken in carriages up the Corkscrew Hill. Black Head is about eight kilometres along the sea-road from Ballyvaughan, heading out toward the Atlantic, a high point of land from which Galway Bay spreads out below. Guarding the entrance to the bay are the Aran Islands, which are visible from Black Head, the nearest only two kilometres or so across the water, a crossing that appears deceptively easy. But the islands used to be cut off in winter and are still infrequently visited now in that season, so treacherous are the reefs and so ferocious and unexpected the storms. Their coasts have seen many a wrecked ship picked clean like the skeleton of a whale.

I recall those winter storms well from my two visits to Ballyvaughan, separated by several years, for the month of December. I stayed both times in the attic of the old, nineteenth-century lifeguards' boathouse, owned by Catherine and Brendan O'Donohue. It was but a short distance across Pier Road to the sea. The stairway to the attic is outside the building at one end, but at the bottom of those stairs I could peer through small windows into the cavernous space where the lifeboats were once kept, the sliding doors facing the sea. It was in the attic of the lifeguard boathouse, on my second visit to Ballyvaughan, that I began writing a book about John Milton. When the storms raged, as they did much of the time, it sounded as if the air and the sea were at war, howling above and roaring below, the rain coming down not in torrents but in hard, soaking sheets, like a giant hand slapping the roof. In one direction on Pier Road is O'Loghlen's Whiskey Pub and then the centre of the village, with the church, St John's, the post office, the Spar grocery shop, and the home of the painter Manus Walsh, whose landscapes catch that sudden illumination which deepens the sense of mystery of this land.

In the other direction on Pier Road, a short way from the village centre, is Monks Pub, where I often went to sit by the turf fire with a Guinness and ate the most delicious mussels in Ireland.

I have attended two midnight masses at Christmas in Ballyvaughan church, where a noble stained glass window by Manus Walsh recapitulates in its design the sea, the shoreline, the rocky plains, the hills and the sky. The window commemorates a great benefactor of the community, and the founder of the Burren College of Art, the late Michael Greene. At the point in the mass when the words of Christ at the Last Supper are spoken – of the bread and later of the wine – the priest spoke in a language that was strange to me, and for an instant I thought, 'Can this be Aramaic?' Then I realised it was Gaelic, the language I saw everywhere on street signs, and had occasionally heard in the pubs. For people in the west of Ireland, even those who do not speak it fluently, Gaelic is one of the finest languages in the world, the natural speech of poets. Like the event the mass celebrates, the sound of the Irish language during the first minutes of Christmas day, as I was anticipating a glass at O'Loghlen's, was a reversal contrary to expectation.

Castle Restoration

Brian Hussey

One morning in early spring, in the second half of the sixteenth century, a woman and her husband were inspecting the progress of a building project. The site was south of Ballyvaughan and north of Lisdoonvarna and had contained the imposing but ruined remains of a large thirteenth-century building. That building had fallen and its walls, where they still stood, were to be part of a new tower house. The woman and the man were aware that when this old establishment had flourished, it had been the centre of a matriarchal community which governed the farms, the fishing, the trading, even the rule of law, in that corner of North Clare.

More importantly, the community was the guardian of an egalitarian, non-violent, earth-centred culture. Its language, its arts, its myths and its music had their roots in a consciousness of a space in its psyche where belief and disbelief, east facing and west facing, domination and submission, the material world and the other world, youth and age, life and death, were coeval and equal.

That space had had great presence and a vitality drawn from a source that had welled up for millennia. In the thirteenth century, the community was aware that their epoch was approaching its end. What had been renewed for centuries was now running out. The flow of its energy was weakening. Even in North Clare, it was moving aside in favour of a new culture with its seat further to the east in Europe. Even though the old culture had an accommodation with early Christianity, it would be written out of history. The victors would erase it from memory.

Máire O'Loughlin and her husband knew all this. They knew the pain that had been felt by participants of the old culture as they saw what they had revered replaced by brash modern authoritarian certainties. The process was slow, its pace measured in centuries. It was illustrated in the earlier oversized, over-elaborate temples like those in Chartres, Paris and Rouen which had vulgar notions of the separation of the 'saved' and the 'damned' represented on their facades, replacing the old simple Christianity. They saw these for what they were – part of an unsubtle modern marketing strategy. At their own place, the O'Loughlins had an eloquent stone head showing a woman from the old culture in despair at what the approaching centuries would bring.

For this culture the collapse of their principal building would have been seen as prophetic, even as a symbol of the power of the feminine giving way to pedestrian masculine reason, but the feminine power long outlived its buildings. It was still strong in Clare into the twentieth century. A hundred years ago there were not too many houses that would risk offending the other world, for example by doubting the power of the fairies.

The same power was alive in Máire O'Loughlin. On the morning in question she addressed Cathal O'Loughlin, 'What sort of a bloody man are you at all? It's eight years now since you said you'd build me a tower like the O'Briens have over in Ballynagowan. What do we have? This bloody shell about eight slats off the ground with a half paved floor and with no walls around it. Do you want to disgrace us all entirely? What the hell put it in your mind to try to build a grand fire surround when it is technically well beyond your capacity? I'm telling you now this floor is to have walls and a roof before the end of this summer or there will be more than words thrown at you. In the meantime you can sleep in the spare room and you'll stay there until the tower is finished.'

Cathal O'Loughlin was a mild man. He was wise enough to be aware of the powers on which his wife could draw. He had no wish to be exposed to the penalties she could impose, non-violent all right, but the fairies, if they were crossed, had ways to reduce a man to, well, impotence.

He set to work. By August, there had been remarkable progress. There were stairs, a roof, two vaults, three walls, and whitewash had been applied. The fourth wall was the problem.

'Didn't I tell you,' said the woman, 'that bloody fire surround was beyond you?'

Cathal sometimes referred to Máire as 'the woman'. The faint jest masked his acceptance of the old ways.

'If you are not out of here by Michaelmas you will take the consequences and they will be mickle,' she said.

Cathal was a pragmatist. There were things in his life, or there had been, which he cherished. He redoubled his efforts. By 25 September only the last stones for the west wall and the right hand of the vertical of the fire surround, which was to be bevelled, remained to be done – these had to come from the quarry. By 28 September, the quarry had not delivered.

'Lads,' said Cathal, 'build up the fire surround with these rubble stones we had for the outside wall. It might satisfy the woman.'

As it happened the quarry delivered on 29 September, so in order to finish on time the bevelled stones were incorporated into the outside wall.

It is believed that the woman was content at having had her way. It is also believed that Cathal returned from the spare room though this is not known with any certainty.

As in the case of all historical writing, it is appropriate to use sources. The events herein described took place at Gregan Castle. That was the name of the place then, as it is now.

I cannot vouch with total confidence for every part of this account. Towards the end of the twentieth century, I did carry out some repairs at the castle and found the bevelled stones in the west outside wall and the rubble stones in the fire surround. I put the stones in their correct places – after all one cannot be too careful. The spirit of the place retains its feminine character. Cathal O'Loughlin obeyed it. It might have been foolish, even dangerous, to do otherwise. It is safer to avoid testing its remaining strength.

Tales

The Young Christy
Mary and Christy Hayes

My grandfather used to have the roads contract and I'd help him after school. I was only a young fellow then. In the 1950s it was, or thereabouts. We'd be up working along by Paddy Nolan's. You'd go to Paddy's about 1 p.m. He wouldn't be there but his door was never locked. You'd find the fire raked over and the kettle hanging over it. You'd go down to the shed and search around and you'd find the eggs. Then up to the kitchen. The bacon would be hanging there, you would take it down and cut off a few slices, and there you had a fine meal. You would leave everything as found and be off again.

One time even earlier, I must have been only about eight, I went with Paddy in the pony and trap to the races in Kilfenora. She was like a member of the household that pony, a lovely black colour she was. But I remember in Kilfenora Paddy got terribly drunk and the neighbours just rolled him in the back of the trap and then they put me in and closed the door. They just wrapped the straps around and sent the pony off for home. That animal took the correct turn at every crossroads, and there were about four of them. At one stage the bloke Davoren came and looked into the trap and said to me, 'Well, you look all

Main Street, Ballyvaughan, in the 1970s
© Pat Browne

The Fountain, Ballyvaughan, in the 1970s
© Pat Browne

right but I can't say the same for Paddy.' So we went on anyway and she stopped at the gate for me to open it. I could barely get out the back. I opened the gate and she stood there until I closed it and then she went right to the back door. I couldn't do anything for her, like undoing the straps and letting her out of the trap. I was barely able to get Paddy out and into the house. I went up to bed in the garret. When I got up in the morning Paddy was outside with his arms around the pony, telling her how sorry he was for leaving her outside without water or hay or anything. You wouldn't meet cars then. There were no lights on the traps but the animals were like that in those days. They could always find their way home.

Later I worked for the Electricity Supply Board. In the 1970s and into the 1980s we worked all over Connemara and parts of Mayo. We were often out there in the middle of the night and at break of day. Then you'd see the houses, trees and mountains all reflected in the lakes. It was fantastic. I really enjoyed that work and we all got on well together.

We used to play cards a lot back then. If you cheated you were not wanted. You learned that fast. Years and years ago we were up playing in Lisdoonvarna. Harry Irwin was there and his uncle, Máirtín Óg, and it was a serious tournament and money was involved. Well, our team got into the final against a crowd from way beyond Liscannor; one of them was a real tough-looking fellow with a cap on the side of his head. I was only watching. It came to the very last lift for the money and this fella stood up and he hit a great bang on the table with his card and shouted, 'There's nothing to beat my four of diamonds!' I was watching Máirtín Óg and I saw him gesture that he had nothin' up his sleeve. Now there were about forty cards lying there and he stood up and shouted, 'What about

Main Street, Ballyvaughan, today
© Karin Funke

The Fountain, Ballyvaughan, today
© Karin Funke

my six?' and with that he hit the table and half the cards in the deck went on the floor and he knew the six must have been there. No one could dispute him. He was beside Harry in the van coming home and Harry says to him, 'Tell the truth, you bastard, did you have that six?'

'Where would I get it?' was the reply and there was great laughter.

But Máirtín Óg knew his cards and knew the six was still in the pack.

There were the stories we had too, hauntings and that. I saw something myself, down where the cholera hospital used to be. 'Twas a wintery night and a person was standing there and I passed and said, 'Goodnight.' There was no answer so I said it again. Still no answer. I looked back then and there was no one there at all – she'd gone. I was fierce uneasy. When I got to the house, I went to my grandfather. He was in bed and I told him.

'Now, Christy,' he said, 'go down now again and search …'

'Jesus, I'm not doing that.'

'Search again, Christy, for your own peace of mind.'

I found nothing but it was awful eerie. Then I thought it was a woman who used to go into Vaughan's for milk. So I went down to her house but she'd been sick all day in bed, never stirred out at all. That finished me altogether. I mightn't have minded but a year before that I laughed at a fellow who said he'd seen a maid, all ghostly-like, there. There were huge numbers of sightings like that. Sometimes there was an explanation, sometimes none.

There was very little money back then and an awful lot of emigration. They were going all the time. The poor old folk used to be mighty sad. But 'twasn't all sad. We had dances, singing and music, and at Christmas time we'd all dress up and do the Wren Boys. We'd go from house to house and we'd dance a figure of a set in them. We'd be dancin' round the table, it would be set for the dinner, and you could always swipe the odd potato. We'd dance all night if we were let. We didn't want much. When Johnny Vaughan got married, the celebrations went on for three days. There was a man, Máirtín, who said, 'All I want is my tin of Woodbines [cigarettes] and a pint.' And my own grandfather said you were all right, 'If you have a little bit to eat and a roof over your head and a bit of fire.' They lived a different life altogether, they did.

Fun and wit
Doreen and Bernie Comyn

Paddy Timmins was very witty. He was walking one day when a car stopped by him. Paddy had never seen the driver. He asked Paddy, 'Is this the right road to Lisdoonvarna, Paddy?'

The reply came fast, 'How do you know Paddy is my right name?'

'Oh, I just knew,' replied the driver.

'Then by the same token you know the *right* road to Lisdoonvarna.'

When the rental thatched cottages were built at the end of the 1960s and it got about that there was underfloor heating in them, Jacko O'Connor remarked, 'That'll keep the rats warm.'

The same Jacko, on seeing a cart piled with straw with a man on the top, said, 'There's a big rat on the straw – that'll change the breed.'

Paddy Connolly tells a story of two men who got electricity

Bernie Comyn performing at Hyland's Hotel, Ballyvaughan
© *Pat Browne*

in their house in the late 1950s. One brother said to the other, 'That light is too dazzling. I'll turn it down.'

He went over to the switch and pulled it down thinking that would dim the light. It put them in the dark all right.

JIM ROUNDS UP THE TALES
Jim Hyland

When I look back on my early youth, I realise how lucky I was being born and reared in a business premises, Hyland's Hotel and shop. It brought me into constant touch with the many older people who made up the marvellous tapestry of village life. One larger than life character was the village blacksmith, Thady O'Loghlen, known to all as Gundy. His forge was in a part of our building so I felt I had more of a right than most urchins to 'help' Gundy. He loved Guinness and his language to his customers was often very flowery, but people understood him and there was no resentment. We named the main restaurant in our family hotel after Thady – the Gundy Room.

Another delightful character was known as Tomás an Asal (Thomas the Ass). Without fail, Tomás invaded the village each Thursday for the market. He announced his arrival on the outskirts by braying like a donkey, and he was so good that all the donkeys, about twenty, began to bray also – a choir. Tomás' arrival caused chaos and uproar. He was not too popular with other donkey owners.

Aut (Austin) Kerin from nearby Carron was a frequent visitor to Ballyvaughan. He walked the distance over the mountains. He always dressed in black from boots to hat. He'd spend the day in our bar telling stories and drinking Guinness. Then he'd be off home again walking over the pitch-black hills. He never missed the annual pilgrimage to Croagh Patrick. He walked there from his home, climbed the Reek and then walked home.

Martin Keane, a farmer and horseman, was a fine man. He could always be called on for help, no problem being too much, sick animals, mares foaling, even breaking in young horses. He could also drink Guinness.

One evening a local farmer was in the bar drinking with Gene Kelly, the film star and dancer. The farmer hadn't a notion who Gene was and they talked about farming and horses. Then the six-o'clock news came on the television so they listened. After the news, a Gene Kelly film was shown. The farmer looked from Gene in the film to the Gene beside him and at last said, 'Well only you're sitting there beside me I'd say that was you, but sure a man can't be in two places at once.'

Paddy Keane lived in a tiny house known as 'Te' or 'Tay Lane'. The name was probably derived from Paddy's attempt to set up a tea manufacturing plant in his house. He used a local herb called 'Maurig Rine' found all over the Burren, which he collected and dried. He then used a secret formula which he would never divulge, but in spite of the scarcity of tea during the Second World War, Paddy's tea was not a success. Paddy suffered from war wounds inflicted at the Somme but he considered himself luckier than many who never came home.

In 1942 just before Christmas, an American fighter aircraft crash-landed on a sandbank at Harbour Hill near the Rine in Ballyvaughan. There were no casualties. The village was full of people shopping for Christmas so there was tremendous excitement and within hours the military arrived to secure the scene. I remember seeing the pilot sitting in O'Loghlen's sitting-room (now Monks Pub). He was dressed in a leather, fleece-lined jacket. To us children he seemed like a man from outer space. Then the army blew up the plane. Souvenir hunters descended on the wreckage. I believe the wheels are still to be seen in a local house.

At Poll Salach

Easter Sunday, 1998

Michael Longley

While I was looking for Easter snow on the hills
You showed me, like a concentration of violets
Or a fragment from some future unimagined sky,
A single spring gentian shivering at our feet.

In Search of the Megalithic Quarry

(A tribute to Paul Carter and the Burren)

Ré Ó Laighléis

May Day. The foot falls lightly on the rock. Craggy Burren limestone, burnt from grey to white by a high and hanging midday sun. A crossing of the stone divide that serves as threshold between the world of the banal and that of the spirits, of migrant imagination, of the perpetual, the mesmerically old. Páirc na Binne – field of the peak – open to be seen, seen to be walked, walked to be savoured.

Páirc na Binne – known to me only for its huge and ever-towering megalithic tomb that straddles this and other worlds. Its gigantic capping stone, perched on half-high orthostats, as impressive as ever I had found it on any one of a thousand previous visits. The vestigial remains of a one-time earthen cover atop the capping stone, kaleidoscopically parading a splendid floral boast of early summer. Who left us this? Who were these people so knowing of what lies beyond?

'Let's move,' says the carterman, who has brought me here.

'What?' I respond, my musing on what may or may not have been some millennia ago disrupted by his speech.

'Westward,' he says, looking at me in benign authority, the prospect of wonders-yet-to-be-seen discernible in his gaze, and a seasoned nod suggesting that he knows what he's about. 'West by south-west,' he says, 'let's go.' And we move on.

He is of the silent type, sparing in his use of words, the carterman. Silent when that is as he wants it. Silent, too, even when he might rather have it otherwise. An Englishman and more, far more. Seasoned by seventy summers. Something in his make-up tells me that he could cast much more than a little light on those brethren who stood and planted stone on stone 5,000 years before. But a mortal such as I will not be rendered privy to such secrets. I sense that he himself is of them. He goes ahead of me across the limestone floor and I watch his every move. Careful in his footing, never of an ilk to surrender himself to the darkened depths of a gaping gryke, mischievously created by nature where two huge spreads of rock never could agree to be as one.

The sun has made its own of the carterman's long, flowing silver hair. Hair and sun, sun and hair, impossible to tell apart. He is definitely one of their number. Grey God of the stone. Everything about him suggests that it is so.

'Pine marten,' he announces, his index finger pointed towards a rock, then he moves on. I look where he has indicated: a dark brown-coloured turd sits proudly on the rock. How does he know that this is what it is? I am just about to ask when he deigns to speak again.

'Look.' Again he points, this time to a hillock to the south-west. The finger's middle joint is craggy and wrinkled, just like the rock itself. And I look. A huge tomb. Its dark, yawning mouth, though distant from us, invites us to come closer.

'A gap,' the carterman observes, and my eye follows the

direction of his gaze to where a distant wall dips almost to nothingness.

The old man fights for breath as we near the hilltop. His last few steps are all of struggle, but pride defeats the challenge. He slumps down by the tomb and, as if part of that very movement, simultaneously extricates a map from his backpack and spreads it widely on the limestone floor.

'A wedge tomb,' he declares, his announcement more a ploy to buy recuperative time than anything else. I walk around the grave, accommodating my companion in his composure-gathering. A light breeze rises to assist him in his effort. Then he inspects the grave, issuing words of well-won wisdom as he circles this miracle in stone. Again, his right hand dips into the backpack and this time reappears bearing a compass.

'The megalithic quarry,' he says, 'directly due west from here.' West! Where *he* looks, I look. Yet another wall of Burren stone to cross. Our journey's end, our venture's quest: to find this megalithic quarry, whatever it may be. Megalithic quarry! Even the very term has bemused us since hearing of it some days back.

'What do you think it may be?' I ask, then quickly add a suggestion or two in the hope of loosening his tongue.

'Who knows?' he replies, and nothing more is said.

The cackle of craggy scree clacks against the rock when the carterman's trailing leg first brushes the upper stones of the wall, then follows him across it. There is a music that is of the rock. Stone-on-stone, rock-on-rock, scree-on-scree – a cacophony of limestone sound.

A plain of barren stone spreads itself before us, even further than the eye can see. There is nothing to suggest that our quest has not been in vain. But wisdom and patience are lines etched equally on my companion's rugged face.

'Over there,' he says, nodding. I look, then follow him again, taking every care to plant each footstep on the very spot from which his foot has just been lifted.

Then, suddenly, some one hundred paces ahead, a magic opens to us. We stand, mouths agape, eyes as wide as any gap in walls of stone, and our hearts doing things that break the rhythm in our bodies.

'I don't believe it,' I say, the words somehow involuntarily issuing themselves. A tomb so incredibly large that it defies even the wildest imagining of a dreamer's mind. 'The Burren's mega-megalithic tomb,' I declare.

'Yes,' the fellow-traveller stoically replies, and then moves towards it.

We are hardly conscious of the limestone paving underfoot as we approach the tomb. Our movement is more akin to floating than anything more solidly defined.

'Bicameral,' the carterman observes, and he caresses the broad, bright capping stone. It is difficult to visually separate them: carterman-and-stone, stone-and-carterman; stone-and-stone; stone. Greyness of hair and greyness of rock equally regarded beneath a non-discerning sun ... each craggy, each scree-like, each benignly of the vestigial.

'It isn't there, this grave,' my companion announces, and, when I turn towards him, I see that he is on his hunkers, the map already spread for scrutiny again. I look over his shoulder and follow the passage of his weathered finger along the map lines. He's right: it isn't there. And yet, a gliding glance back towards the structure demotes imagination, and reality impresses itself on me again.

'It isn't there,' the carterman reasserts, and his smile broadens in celebration of the victory of the spiritual over the tangible. He sits back against one of the side slabs of the grave, presses himself so hard against it that it is difficult to think that they are not one. I look towards the grave yet again and, though my eyes tell me it is there, my mind, my soul, my spirit tell me otherwise.

'You are right, old-timer,' I say, 'it simply isn't there.'

Time to sit, time to think, time for peace of mind. Our eyes comb the barren, windswept limestone surface. If truth is truth, we have found a tomb that isn't there. And yet, if map and truth are truth, a megalithic quarry of repute is lost to us. If truth is truth! A megalithic quarry!

Megalithic quarry. The sun eases itself low in the western sky. The colour amber owns the skin on the carterman's face. He holds his head high, his eyes flitting from place to place, their pupils casting Apollo's rays back onto the rock. The dignity of the old-timer, the wisdom, the depth. His otherness unsettles me. I stir, flustering with the map, gathering, folding, compelling myself to break a silence that has rendered me uneasy.

'Quiet,' my comrade says. There is an authority in his voice that is beyond the human. I quieten and look at him. He is riveted to the rock on which he sits, his stare fixed hard on something in the distance. I lean forward and look into his eyes, and there, in his deep dilated pupils, stands an army of broad grey capping stones, each and every one of them propped by a lesser rounded stone and ready for use. Hundreds of them, thousands, maybe. All washed in the gleaming colour amber.

'Over yonder,' he says, 'the quarry.'

As though outside himself, the old one stands and moves

with the breeze towards that place on which his eyes are fixed. I follow in his path, drawn by a force that I cannot identify.

'The megalithic quarry,' the carterman declares, and tears are shed. And, in every tear that's shed, a big, broad stone falls from the pupils of his eyes and lays itself bare on the limestone floor beneath us. The tears fall in their hundreds, thousands. Thousands of tears shedding themselves in stone. And, when all his tears are cried, the expanse of pavement is strewn with capping stones, every single one of them propped up by a lesser rounded stone. Each one lies gaping, luring, primed for the use for which it has been readied. They lie as old, as worked, as weighty as the very tombs themselves.

'They are for us,' the carterman tells me, and his eyes are not the eyes of the human world.

No return journey is made, this day of stone. Not another wall is crossed. Foot falls to rock even more lightly than the lightest footing. And the carterman – he has vanished without trace. A light breeze that is as silent as it is sparing blows hauntingly around the world of Páirc na Binne.

Burren Prayer

Michael Longley

Gentians and lady's bedstraw embroider her frock.
Her pockets are full of sloes and juniper berries.
Quaking-grass panicles monitor her heartbeat.
Her reflection blooms like mudwort in a puddle.
Sea lavender and Irish eyebright at Poll Salach,
On Black Head saxifrage and mountain everlasting.
Our Lady of the Fertile Rocks, protect the Burren.
Protect the Burren, Our Lady of the Fertile Rocks.

The Green Road

Stephen Ward

Where the Green Road leaves the coast road it is hemmed in by walls of rounded cobbles interlaced with brambles and ivy. At first, it is navigable by vehicles serving dwellings, holiday homes and farms. The fields to either side, which once would have been cut for hay, are speckled red with clover and yellow with buttercups. It is a warm June day with swallows twittering overhead and a cuckoo calling in the distance, but peat stacked beside a wall by the main road hints at winter. By the last house, there is a large vegetable plot with potatoes and leeks.

Looking down, the coastal plain has expanses of bare rock, pastures, low grassy hills and sand dunes. White houses are dotted here and there. The fields in which cattle and sheep are grazing have bushy margins for shelter. In one field stand long-necked animals – some white, others brown – a herd of llamas.

From this point on, the Green Road becomes a path. A newly built stile leads into a field where, until recently, the old road was impassable. Now cleared of scrub, enormous boulders bear scratches where the excavator re-arranged them. Willow warblers flit among the whitethorn and a recently fledged robin eyes its surroundings.

The Green Road is a limestone road. Underfoot, limestone is exposed which once formed the floor of a tropical sea. To either side are limestone walls; in places these are built of loose stone but over large stretches they consist of enormous blocks laid on their sides long ago. The thin turf is burned brown in places; where it is rooted in deeper soil it is still green, sometimes indicating where long straight crevices separate the larger blocks of underlying rock. Beyond the wall, a pair of magpies draw attention to a fox with raucous calls. The fox disappears, drawn perhaps towards a flock of starlings which flew beyond it. Beside the track nods quaking grass; earlier in the year it was here that gentians lit the turf. Today, the flashes of blue are the tiny skirts of milkwort. Sea plantain in the turf might go unnoticed as grass, and it is hereabouts, in the vestigial pockets of soil in the limestone hollows, that Norwegian sandwort went undiscovered until 1961 and then sank back into anonymity until spotted by a sharp-eyed botanist in 2008. Locally, it is becoming known as Fanore sandwort!

Conspicuous by their size are limestone boulders, the occasional one taller than a man; arriving here many millennia ago, they now sit where left by melting ice. How far they have come is uncertain, but adjacent to the sea a mile or so south of Black Head there is one of granite which must have come from the far side of Galway Bay. Until recent days, the turf surrounding the largest limestone boulder was speckled yellow with the delicate wind-blown flowers of hoary rockrose. Small heath butterflies fly over the grassland, landing every now and then, giving a glimpse of orange and brown before they are off again. Just as active, but much more conspicuous, are common blue butterflies – a lovely shade of powder blue, the females flecked with orange.

Heathland distinguished by the dark foliage of ling and the shiny green of mountain avens occupies large areas. With one or two exceptions, the mountain avens are past flowering, most heads now being capped by a twirl of feathery seeds, but the occasional one still has eight white petals, surrounding a ring of yellow stamens and a centre of greenish stigmas. Its tiny leaves are dark green above but covered in a white felt below – a means perhaps of limiting water loss. Whitish-green flowering spikes of lesser butterfly orchid abound where the soil is damper. To the east are limestone pavements and low cliffs, rising to the high Burren. Up out of sight, a skylark is singing and meadow pipits complete their song by displaying their flying skills in a carefully controlled descent. From the mountain comes the deep call of a raven. Sentinel atop some bushes is that most characteristic of Burren birds, the stonechat, with its distinctive black head, white cheek, orange breast and staccato call which resembles two stones being struck together; on occasion the male gives a short song and display flight. Cowpats indicate that cattle do graze up here, but none are to be seen today. Dictated by shortage of water up here in summer, this is winterage, i.e. grazed in winter. All the cattle are on the more easily watered, lusher grassland below.

The sky is mainly cloud-covered but with patches of the palest blue. The mountains of Connemara stand out clearly but seem to be lent colossal height by the intervening sea being swathed in mist. The coastal plain is fringed brown with seaweed. Ahead, the Burren can be seen to be built of layers of limestone. Beside the track grow two or three whitethorns; topiaried by the Atlantic gales, all their growth is directed inland, although today the air is so still that the predominant sound is that of a bumblebee.

A small copse of hawthorn by the road has its own bird life: a blackbird is singing, a wood pigeon clatters away and the bushes seem alive with recently fledged birds – blue tits, willow warblers and robins. The track is becoming rockier, with a low cliff flanking the landward side. In the crevices grow those ferns which specialise in rocky places – wall rue, maidenhair spleenwort, hart's-tongue and others. A wheatear and his mate are prospecting for a nest site; as they fly, a flash of white above the tail draws attention to them – wheatear is said to derive from this distinctive white flash. Once much more common, these birds winter in Africa, and breed in Ireland and elsewhere in northern Europe. Closely related to the stonechat, they make a similar call.

From the summit, the track falls to the north as if about to plummet into Galway Bay. As it does so, it swings round from a northerly to an easterly direction. Below is the sea – a deep turquoise seen from up here – with the distinctive screech of the occasional sandwich tern fishing below clearly carried aloft. Ahead lies Finavarra with its Martello tower and eventually the fields of Gleninagh, dotted with grazing cattle and sheep. Beyond is Ballyvaughan backed by the white limestone hills of Abbey Hill, Ucht Máma and Moneen. These northern slopes are scattered with whitethorn, willow and rowan and have a more luxuriant heath, dominated by ling, with mountain avens and the magenta flowers of bloody cranesbill in abundance. This damper slope better suits twayblade with its spikes of little green men and that loveliest of orchids, *Gymnadenia*, combining beauty and fragrance. Water seepages have purple moor-grass and black bog-rush, amongst which are the bright-green 'starfish' of butterwort, the tiny pink flowers of bog pimpernel, purple and white columbine and – the most intriguing flower in the shape of an insect – the bee orchid, with its pink petals and brown, mottled labellum.

As the track descends, it becomes increasingly hemmed in by whitethorn, ivy, bracken and bramble, but again recent clearance has been effective in preventing the route becoming impassable. Speckled wood butterflies dance between the hedges. Whilst not yet complete, the intention would seem to be to re-establish a through-route to Gleninagh – a most welcome move in adapting this ancient route to a new role.

Returning to Murrogh, the ice-scoured northern flank of the Burren presents a steep, smooth limestone face to Galway Bay. Turning the corner to head south, the sea mist has cleared to reveal the Aran Islands strung out along the horizon; Inis Mór and Inis Meáin appear as one, but Inis Oírr is clearly separated by a strait. The sea has the look of beaten metal but is patterned with smoother lanes and channels. On the far horizon, sea and sky merge.

To walk the Green Road is to connect with the past. Just when did man first travel this way? In some places the road is cut into the rock, in others it has been engineered as a shelf on the mountainside; along its whole length substantial walls flank it. Even though most goods were probably transported by sea, before the modern coast road was constructed this was clearly a significant route. Today it has a new role: from it walkers can see the Burren, its wild flowers and birds, whilst also enjoying distant glimpses of Connemara and the Aran Islands and, at the same time, getting away from busy modern roads.

Moneen Mountain Moves?

Paul Carter

Morning wakened and going outside
Gentle rain and mist surround.
Looked Atlantic west and eastwards
Wondered if the clouds were breaking
First fag before the lengthy breakfast
Sheltered in the front door entry
'A soft day' being agreed with Bernie
'Not a day for the bed' was also spoken,
Contemplated, considered, accepted.
'The mountain seems near to the house today'
I said, my mind seeking explanation
Ranged around the scattering of light
Water droplets bending the rays,
Would that foreshorten or lengthen
Apparent distance from the mountain?
He too, in silence, sized up the matter.
Next day, a hard wind-driven rain,
'A day for the bed', meaning that nothing
Of use on the land or with cattle
Could be achieved or even started.

Give up. I drove somewhere.
The next a clear sunshiny day.
Warm. The limestone brightly sharp.
He saw me admiring the light on Moneen –
'The mountain's a long way
From the house today.
Get some fresh bread and cheese, fill up your flask now,
Get off as soon as you can.'
Since then, every now again,
Depending on what the weather's doing,
The right remark on the moveable mountain
He repeats, as if my aim were to climb.
At Lough Rask, west of Moneen,
Lives Bernie Comyn, maker of myths.

Joy on a Road to Ballyvaughan

Carmel Cunningham

The intense blue of the spring gentian
Hits the heart with its beauty.
The wonder of the delicate mountain avens
Spreading over limestone rock
Causes the soul to smile.
The richness of the bloody cranesbill
Pulsating with colour,
Sometimes finding shelter in the limestone grykes,
But living happily on grassy heaths,
Fills the mind with warmth.
The excitement of finding one's first
Full-flowered orchid.
The creamy-white of the burnet rose
In rocky places.
The pale green fan-shaped leaves
Of the maidenhair fern, living happily
In the limestone cracks.
The first sight of the road
That circles round Black Head,
The colours of the shimmering sea

On the way to Ballyvaughan
And peace in the bustling village,
Cosmopolitan yet rural,
Offering city treats in little places,
Where friends are never strangers,
And strangers become friends.

Ballyvaughan before 1914
© *Lawrence Collection, Courtesy of the National Library of Ireland*

In Aillwee Cave

Michael Longley

There must be grazing overhead, hazel thickets,
Pavements the rain is dissolving, springs and graves,
Darkness above the darkness of the seepage of souls
And hedges where goosegrass spills its creamy stars.

Vocation

Micheal O'Siadhail

Ní féidir leis an ngobadán an dá thrá a fhreastal
A sandpiper cannot tend two shores

Yes, of course, Kierkegaard was right:
Purity of heart is to love one thing.

For twenty helter-skelter years a niggling
Of too little done before the gentle night.

Brown-backed white-bellied wader
Teetering hurriedly between two shores.

Too tired after those day-job chores;
A muse's overwhelmed serenader.

Then the gift and scope of another shore
To wade wherever a tidal rip demands.

A bobbing, nodding head in the sands.
A sandpiper busy on a single shore.

If you run after two hares, you will catch neither

My father's whispering I recall
Pity too damned intense, too hyper,
Hunting every hare he can.

On our island once the sandpiper.
But across a landmass to Japan
Deux lièvres, zwei Hasen, Nito.

Lesson one for any huntsman.
Only a fool would ever go
Running after two hares at once.

This easy smiling *bon mot*
Of knowing fathers warning sons
How quickly hares go to ground.

Dream-chaser I stick to my guns,
Run with hare, hunt with hound.
O no *mon père* I'll catch them all.

En kan ikke ri to hester samtidig
(One cannot ride two horses at one time)

To travel overland to Trondheim
Or bring good news
From Ghent one horse at a time.
But yes that red-bloused circus rider
Astride two horses
Reining the gap when it spilt wider

Over the haltered here and there
Applause endorses
Between the saddle and the giddy air
And fallen for the wonder of a ring
I couldn't choose
Either the moment or its beckoning
When rein and rhythm correspond
In sway and rhyme.
    Sweet here. Sweet beyond.

The Burren – A Birder's Paradise

George Keegan

> O Blythe new-comer! I have heard,
> I hear thee and rejoice.
> O Cuckoo! Shall I call thee Bird,
> Or but a wandering Voice?
> While I am lying on the grass
> Thy twofold shout I hear,
> From hill to hill it seems to pass,
> At once far off, and near.
> (William Wordsworth: *To the Cuckoo*)

One of the attractions for me when deciding to move to Ballyvaughan permanently was undoubtedly the diverse and varied selection of birds it is possible to observe in the Burren throughout the year. Birds have inspired me throughout my life, from my early youth growing up in the south Monaghan town of Carrickmacross when I was fascinated by the call of the corncrake in a small meadow close to the grass tennis court in the town. I am still fascinated to the present day. I have always found it exhilarating, watching birds in their natural habitat.

At the outset I must point out that my knowledge is adequate, not encyclopaedic. I will therefore attempt to give readers a short account of the birds I have seen on a regular basis through the seasons, a few good locations for birdwatching, a short list of some rare birds discovered in recent years and some special moments for me.

While there are four seasons in the year, when it comes to birdwatching I am inclined to divide the year into three: winter, spring, summer. My wife, Mary, and I are fortunate to live close to the seafront, which enables us, particularly during the winter months when the village is quiet, to watch a mix of wader ducks from the kitchen window. Among the species to be seen daily are Brent geese, mergansers, widgeon, redshank, curlews, cormorants, grey herons, gulls, crows, starlings and a pair of mute swans who reside here all year round. Occasionally a lone great northern diver also arrives on the incoming tide to feed.

As I move around the Burren, it is possible to see several hundred widgeon and teal at Loch Muirí, close to the Flaggy Shore and on the turloughs (vanishing lakes). Bell Harbour has dozens of waders, such as dunlin, sanderlings and oystercatchers, and ringed plover can be seen at the Rine (Ballyvaughan). When the wind blows up a storm, out I go with binoculars and telescope to Black Head to view passing seabirds driven close to land by the wind. Auks, petrels and shearwaters can all be observed and there is always the possibility of seeing a storm petrel. This is also a good place to watch a gannet plunge into the sea for food. I also find redwing or fieldfare feeding in the fields and along hedges as I drive the winter roads.

In complete contrast, late spring and summer bring bustle and noise to the villages, with speedboats and other craft on

Burren robin
© *Beth O'Connell*

the sea. Then it is time to head for the hills and valleys of our wonderful Burren. Here the flora and fauna are breathtaking. One good way to observe birds is to let them come to you. On many a warm spring or summer evening, I have spent several hours hoping to see a badger family or the elusive pine marten. On these occasions to keep still is essential, and while waiting I have often been entertained by the song of a blackbird, song thrush or robin quite close to me and seemingly unaware of my presence. Another bird I love to watch is the ever-busy long-tailed tit. I see them often on the Green Road at Lismacteige. A couple of times a year a small flock decides to go on a tour around Ballyvaughan. They flit from tree to tree. Other small species in residence at this time of year include stonechats, the somewhat rarer whinchat and various warblers.

One of my favourite spots to go birdwatching is the Caher

valley in Fanore. Here we find the only river that runs over-ground for the whole of its course in the Burren. This is the place to see dippers and grey wagtails. Further up the valley, near Fermoyle, is a great place to hear the cuckoo. Other good places to listen to this bird are Gleninagh, around Fanore and Newtown Castle, Ballyvaughan. Sometimes the grasshopper warbler can be heard close to the forestry area on the way to Lisdoonvarna. The doons at Fanore and Bishop's Quarter are good for skylarks and there are nestings and martins in the latter. Raptors can turn up anywhere and merlin, hen harriers, kestrels, sparrow hawks and peregrines can also be seen. On the Rine, sandwich terns dive for food and there are shell duck and wheatear here. Black guillemots nest between Gleninagh and Black Head Lighthouse. Here too shags roost.

In winter I always look forward to the annual visit to the Rine of a small group of tiny and very attractive snow buntings, usually only four. I find these delightful birds are not as timid as other species and can be viewed at very close range. During the summer of 1997 I was lucky to see two meadow pipits feeding a young cuckoo at Ucht Máma, and a few years ago, on two separate occasions, I was able to watch nesting peregrines. One of the nests was at Aillwee Mountain. It had been taken over by the raptor after a family of ravens had finished nesting. Another memorable time was watching a flock of golden plover while I walked high on Cappanawalla Mountain. Little egrets can now be seen in the Burren.

Noel Walsh, who lives in Fanore, is probably the most knowledgeable bus driver in the country when it comes to birds! He is well known for stopping the bus on occasion to point out to his passengers a bird or animal by the side of the road. It was on one of his routine journeys to Galway several years ago that he spotted a crane feeding at New Quay in the Burren. Other interesting visitors seen by Noel while birdwatching include tree creepers near Ballyvaughan, long-eared owls by his home in Fanore, an osprey hounded by hooded crows up the Caher valley. One of the most unusual rarities was the visit in the 1980s of a belted kingfisher to Ballyvaughan. This brought 'twitchers' from far and wide.

We are fortunate that Gordon D'Arcy lives locally. He has written several books about the area and conducts birdwatching walks for students. He also takes part in the Ballyvaughan and Burren Dawn Chorus Walk during the annual May-time 'Burren in Bloom' festival.

Sadly, some species have dwindled rapidly. One species rarely encountered now is the lapwing. I recall MacNeill O'Loghlen telling me of large flocks of them feeding across from his public house. A chough sighting is now rare, but they used to breed at Gleninagh Castle tower. Conservation and construction work on the castle frightened them away. Some are still seen around Fanore. The heronry at Lough Rask, Ballyvaughan, has disappeared.

Wall Beauty

Carmel Cunningham

Walls of every shape
Moulded with grey stone,
Angled erect, sideways.
Holes for peeking through,
Or through which a bird can fly,
Or frog can hop,
Or crocodile-marching ants
Go about their daily chores.
Separating field from field –
Some filled with meadow flowers and orchids,
Others sparse green with pavements,
More only with clints and grykes
Filled with wonder
Of unexpected treasures –
All singular these dividers,
Some ancient, others young.
Some arthritic, needing
Gentle careful mending
But all so filled with beauty
With limestone gentleness,

The greyness warm, not cold.
Patterned, quirky,
Variable.
Some slightly humped,
Each held together
By clever assembling,
Moulded to look simple,
Yet remaining upright and proud
And spirited,
As if just now erected
In the marvel of that special place,
The Burren.

The B&B, 90 Minutes after Sunset

Paul Carter

Eleven thirty outside Comyn's
Turn the key, but look behind.
The ash that's ever late in leafing
Silhouetted on a blue west sky
Graded from a deep tone high
Paler hue towards horizon.
Through the dark dendritic divisions
Of upward outward searching limbs
Two bright stars light-sparkle
On the half dark western night.
Remember don't bring the key.
But if you think you're the last
Turn out the light.

Chris the Guide

Chris & Mick Carrucan with Sarah Poyntz

Chris Carrucan (born in Ballyvaughan) took me on a guided tour of 1940s Ballyvaughan village. She pointed out all the trades and crafts available in those days. The post office was also a drapery. There was another drapery at Peter O'Loghlen's Pub, now Monks Pub. Part of the car park of Hyland's Hotel was a forge run by Gundy, the blacksmith. Baby Mooney's shop was where the town houses are, opposite the petrol station. The butcher ran his shop on the corner of the present crafts centre and the carpenter worked on the corner by the bridge. There were two hotels, the Central and McNamara's, and five dressmakers, one tailor, four postmen, a pension officer, registrar, a dole officer and a midwife (near Clareville). The present renovated St John's Community Hall was the primary school. There was no secondary school. There was a dispensary near the site of the present primary school where the workhouse was once.

It is obvious that in those days Ballyvaughan was a bustling village with most of the trades and crafts that were then needed. Today it has no cobbler, butcher or tailor, nor a registrar, or pensions and dole officers, these two roles having been centralised to a huge government department. The big weekly markets and the annual fairs are now succeeded by an excellent weekly Farmers' Market on Saturday and by a Craft Fair on Sundays. These are held at the renovated St John's Hall. The Ladies' Club of Ballyvaughan was responsible for this restoration in the 1980s and the President of Ireland, Mary Robinson, opened it.

I asked Chris about school in her day and she gave me the following account:

Mrs O'Loghlen taught us. She was a great teacher and taught us to read, write – the three Rs – how to sew, knit and sing. We sang the mass in Latin. Boys and girls were taught together. Mr Long was the second teacher. He played the organ. If it rained on the way to school, we had to sit in our wet clothes all day. We also had to clean the school. The seniors lit the fire. Parents brought turf for the fire. Confirmation classes were held Saturday mornings and there was confirmation every three years. We would make a circle in the churchyard and the bishop would ask each one three questions. If some didn't know the answer they had to wait another three years – it was an awful disgrace if that happened.

Chris' husband Mick added:

After mass on Sundays my uncle played the concertina and others played the tin whistle and the flute for a dance in a neighbour's. 'Twas all house dances in those days. There'd be tea and maybe barm brack.

There were four of us, the three brothers and myself. We always went to the dances together. No sooner would we arrive than someone would shout, 'Clear the floor for the Carrucan brothers.'

Then the priests stopped the house dances, and after that they were held in halls, if there was one. In Ballyvaughan, they were held in a big room in the workhouse and one of the priests attended.

Mick went on to say:

We used to have the American Wakes too. We gathered to wish well to the people going. Most went to the States or to England. We went to England. Most going to America went to Gort railway station, took the train to Limerick, then Cork and Cobh and then the boat to New York. Sad, it was all right.

Chris finished:

The ones going to America had to be claimed by someone living over there. The wake was a kind of mixture of sadness and gladness, sad because of leaving and probably never coming back and glad because the person was claimed and would have a chance, an opportunity. We were lucky: all our children did well in England and we came back.

The Music Man, Chris Droney

Margaret & Chris Droney with Sarah Poyntz

He has delighted the old, the middle-aged and the young with his music. Chris Droney remembers when he was about eight years old, in the first half of the twentieth century, going off on his own into a dark room and playing the notes of his concertina. It is a touching picture of a little boy practising the music he loved and keeping up the traditions of his family – both his father, James, and his grandfather, Michael, were concertina players. He tells us that his left hand was more accurate than his right one – it never missed a note. Since there was no secondary school Chris stayed home at age fourteen to help his father on the farm. So not only was he a musician but he was also a farmer and a good one. Life had to be sustained, survival ensured, but music was and still is a big part of Chris Droney's life.

He played with three other musicians in Johnson's Hall, Kinvara. They were given half a crown each for the session and before they left for home, Johnson's arranged cups of tea and sandwichs for them in O'Grady's Hotel, called Mountain View where the Merriman Hotel is now. They cycled there and back. Chris says that you'd see hundreds of bicycles in the

The Music Man, Chris Droney of Bell Harbour © M. Droney

small towns in those days and there was no need for locks on them. Cars began to be seen in the late 1940s.

One time when Chris was cycling home from a session in Kinvara at about 1 a.m., he heard an awful rattling of chains. He remembered all the stories he'd heard of ghostly figures rattling chains. He nearly died of fright. His fingers tightened on the handlebars. Then he saw a man leading a flock of about fourteen chained goats. He was walking them from Ballyvaughan to Kinvara. He had helped himself to the goats in Ballyvaughan and was going to sell them in Kinvara.

The priests used to go about clearing houses and places unapproved by them of dancers and players. Once a priest came to clear a house and he said to one of the organisers of the dance: 'Wherever there are these dances there's the divil in the place.'

'Well, Father, I've been to these dances all over and I've never met him yet,' replied the organiser.

Chris played in 'The Bell Harbour Ceílí Band' with Jimo Kane, Martin Rabbit and Seán Nilan. The band played in all the local villages, Ballyvaughan, Lisdoonvarna, Gort, Kinvara. At one session in Lisdoonvarna, Chris noticed a lovely girl dancing. She had bobbed hair over one eye. However, he was on stage playing and the band were not allowed off it until they were finished. The interval came and a relative of the lovely girl asked Chris if he'd like a 7UP.

'I will if you can get that girl with the bob over her eye to come up here.' The girl was Margaret. They were married about a year and a half later, the only couple, Chris says, who 'were brought together by 7UP!' It was a marriage where Chris had his wife's full support for both his music and the work of the farm. He played solos all over the world – France, Germany, Spain, Portugal, Greece, England, Scotland, Wales, Isle of Man, Canada, United States – and with Margaret on three Caribbean cruises. It is a delight to Margaret and Chris that their grandson, Daithí, is devoted to traditional music, reaching the final with his fiddle-playing in the All Ireland RTÉ Talent Show.

Margaret began to run a Bed and Breakfast and has only ceased this recently. Both loved to give an old traditional welcome to guests. They had many from abroad who became regular visitors. German teachers who drove a Mercedes came. They loved Chris' music and one day they drove him to Galway airport and flew him out to Inis Mór, in the Aran

The slipway at Bell Harbour
© *Karin Funke*

Islands. They walked around and then the Germans brought him into a pub. They asked him to play and the music started. Gradually many tourists came in and there was a great session. When they returned to Galway airport and the Mercedes they found a large notice on the car, 'WELCOME to IRELAND'. Four teachers from their school had seen the car and had put the notice there. They came over, said they had no place to stay, so they all came back to Bell Harbour House for Bed and Breakfast. Later that day they all, including the Droney family, had champagne and wine and they had a session and danced in the fields. They had a great time.

Margaret and Chris said that no one had much in the early days. There was no electricity. It was all paraffin lamps or candles. Some people had Tilley lamps. They had a double-burner paraffin lamp. Then there was the Rural Electrification Scheme around the 1950s. All the early farm work was done

Old days at Daly's Pub, Bell Harbour
© Rena and Tom Linnane

Daly's Pub today
© Karin Funke

by hand except for threshing machines when it was all tillage around the villages. Margaret remembers milking the cows by hand. She said she was lucky to be able to do this in a shed. Later the milking was all done by milking machine.

Chris could not get his new combine harvester through his gate. He had to leave it outside until the next morning when he had the full light to take the wall holding the gate down.

In 2004 at Fleadh Cheoil na hÉireann in Clonmel, County Tipperary, Chris was presented with the distinction of ÉIGSE by Comhaltas Ceoiltóirí Éireann, the Lifetime Achievement Award for his music playing. His music is of life itself, even the feet of non-dancers keep rhythm to it.

His music for Corcomroe Abbey in Bell Harbour is direct, delicate and touching:

> There is a sacred place 'neath the Burren Mountains
> Where Cistercians came and preached long, long ago
> It's a resting place where lay our forefathers
> In the lonely graves of peaceful Corcomroe.

'Peaceful Corcomroe'
Words and music by Chris Droney

On Cloud Nine

Paul Clements

'Do you think it will thunder?' a rosy-glowed farmer with a lopsided smile once asked me during a mid-morning stroll along a marshy lane on the Black Head road. Leaning over a five-bar steel gate, he sniffed the weather and surveyed the threatening inland sky, a spectacular sight often occurring in the morning, with anvil-topped clouds. Later that afternoon the sky had cleared and the day's drama was complete with the eventual arrival of thunderstorms, although no lightning, by evening.

For twenty years I have flirted with the spirit of the Burren and have frequently considered what has called me back each year. Its clouds and the quality of its light are a source of wonder to me. Visitors often remark on the beauty and colour of the cloud formations that overhang the Burren. With their gradations of tone and exquisite hues, the infinite diurnal variations of clouds know no bounds.

But the Burren clouds and jostling sky with its repertoire of lighting trickery are only one factor that makes me return. There's the light ceaselessly playing tricks with its adjustments throughout the day. It dazzles, flashes, sparkles and glitters on bright days. At other times the light soaks into a pale wash, merging hills, sky and earth so that you can't see the horizon at Black Head. Beams of sun pierce though the sky, spotlighting fields and walls as well as small enclaves of limestone. The acrylic perfection of a sunny day stays long in the memory. The sun, with its repeated appearances and disappearances, acts as a scene-changer. I particularly like the flowering of life in the spring, the way the sunlight spectacularly transmutes the rocks into ever-changing colours, and the constant play of light, through its shape-shifting shadows.

The limestone, chameleon-like, scene-shifts at the whim of the light and weather. One minute an ochrous pink, an hour later a mix of grey and white with sections of the hills plunged into darkness, and later a tint of purple. The Burren hills often seem to bask mildly in the soft, calm air. The ethereal quality of the light – a crepuscular light – often has a bearing on the colours. There are times when the limestone twinkles and scintillates with a shimmering effect across the sedate and mellow landscape. When the sun's rays catch the summit of Cappanawalla, they can reactivate it and make it look as though a flashlight is shining on it.

The Burren possesses what are regarded as the five essential components for finding tranquillity in modern life: natural landscape, birdsong, peace and quiet (a magnificent 'sound'), natural-looking woodland and a star-spangled sky. The daily snapshots and minute dramas of the place – referred to by some writers as 'encounters of meaning' – live long with those who visit it. Incandescent visions of things I've seen often flit across my dreams. Occasionally the commonplace stirs these super-charged, freeze-framed memories, the accumulation of some intense and magical moments. The list with details that are burned on my retina includes the following: a hop, skip and jump over a freshly discovered portion of perfect pavement at Sheshymore; a supernumerary evening rainbow as a momentary backdrop; a cormorant surfacing from the sea and shaking water from its head; seals bobbing up and down in the water at Muckinish; the flash of sunlight on the pavement after rain; jackdaws gathering to soak up the warmth from the limestone; the flight call of a heron; the sight of a solitary figure dropping down the terracing; an upright hare, alert and eager with ears erect reconnoitring the scene; a crow scratching its chin.

The Burren exerts an irresistible pull and I have often tried to account for its centrality in my life. Occasionally I've analysed my own emotions to try and discover why I have such a longing for the place and why I have spent time marinating myself in its mysteries. We all have a collection of images of a place or places that are unquestionably of appeal. Each, in its own way, has at different times of my life, been special. But when I think of where I *really* want to be for supreme happiness, then it is pavement-pounding, tramping the hills, breathing the crystalline air, and indulging in the floral pleasures of the grey limestone. It is a perpetual place, a precious place, a state of mind, an enchantment, a dream place and a dreamer's world. It is a place that weaves an enduring spell with its sights and sounds, its solaces and silences, its sorrows and sadnesses. It enriches and repays those who spend time in it, providing stability and an anchor in a changing world. The ethereal beauty and sense of contentment found there has often called me back. It has been indispensable to my wellbeing, cleansing the toxins and serving my spiritual needs. The American nature writer Richard Nelson puts it well, 'What makes a place special

Martello Tower with Galway city in the background
© *Karin Funke*

is the way it buries itself inside the heart, not whether it's flat or rugged, rich or austere, wet or arid, gentle or harsh, warm or cold, wild or tame. Every place, like every person, is elevated by the love and respect shown toward it, and by the way in which its bounty is received.'

When you are walking the limestone, the outside world can seem a thousand miles away. After each visit, and a renewal of Burren bounty, all is right with the world. To the point of overload, my senses are in a state of heightened awareness, my thirst quenched, my horizons widened. With a revived eye, I feel I can see farther, better appreciate images, shapes and colours, as well as the particularity of small things.

I leave in a happy mental and physical state, content that I can carry around in my head an archive of personal images, and am refreshed with the peace and wildness of it all. Like the paying of a good compliment, the golden afterglow of these images can last up to six months. Its physical finery and visual memory is forever in my mind's eye (partly owing to the fact that a framed folding landscape map, measuring 4ft x 3ft, occupies a huge amount of wall space above my writing desk). It is an essential reference point. If I want to locate quickly Rathborney earth ring, follow the path of the Khyber Pass, check on the cave of St MacDuac hidden away at Keelhilla, put my finger on the twelfth-century churches of Ucht Máma, make sure I've the correct spelling of Cahermacnaghten, or show a visitor where to find the blessed bush and the marks of St Brigid's knees, then all these are instantly accessible … at least from a cartographic point of view. Scan the map and a palimpsest of place names falls mellifluously from the tongue: Lissylishen, Ballyallaban, Tobereenatemple, Lemanagh and Murrough.

So what then is the prevailing spirit of this gentle hill-swaddled stony place at the extreme edge of Europe, and how best can its intrinsic nature be captured? You will never capture the totality of it in words, photographs or painting. You will find it hard to bottle the intoxicating nectar of the Burren for later consumption (an entrepreneur once tried this in Cumbria and sold it in souvenir tins as 'Lake District Air'). The Burren nectar, which is something of an acquired taste, is extremely difficult to pin down. It is an elusive abstraction. Its essential spirit – its *sui generis* – will always remain intangible with its aura of mystery. The Burren holds many secrets. Interpreting its innermost inscrutable thoughts is not an easy challenge. People set out to capture it; instead it captures them.

The wildlife writer Richard Mabey describes it as 'an exuberant, flirtatious landscape'. There is no doubt you could spend a lifetime flirting with the smooth limestone and not do justice to its unending mystery. Yet its essence is to be found everywhere. Catch the right day and you can feel it in the ruins of Corcomroe Abbey or in a walk along a Green Road. You can sense it in the frolic of a large white butterfly on the Flaggy Shore, the swerve of a raven, the quiver of the wind-blown mountain avens, the call of the cuckoo, the pungent smell of three-cornered leek at Gleninagh or in the stalactites hanging in a cave. You can sense it in the exhilaration of the wild waves on a wobbly clint at Poll Salach, during sunset at Black Head, in the curve of a mountain, the feel of the wind coming off the Atlantic, in the shape of a stark erratic with the light ricocheting off it, or an hour spent sea-watching. You can sense it in an evening visit to the Poulnabrone dolmen, a wander through the Rockforest near Mullaghmore on a night of astonishing beauty with a harvest moon of silver quietness when an element of melancholy hangs in the air.

Vignettes from my journal comprising nibble notes, scribbles and loose jottings include a chance meeting with a hare or pine marten, listening to the croak of a frog, watching a red setter run around in circles and then sniff the grass, or glimpsing the flash of a passing shadow. These represent, for me, all that is best, expressing the quintessential excitement and intense pleasure of this energising and life-enriching place. Exploring its enigmas is what makes it special. It is a good place to while away a few hours with your own thoughts and dreams, alone or, if you feel the need, in the company of others. I have come and gone, staying for days, weekends, and weeks on end. I have seen its small dramas of life but have missed much more by not living there. But then, I ask myself, how could I miss it, if I lived there? Many people have visions of a secret home. It could be in the desert, on a mountain top, under the sea, or beside a bog. The tourism PR and travel articles about the Burren sell it as a 'great wilderness', a 'moonscape' or 'lunar landscape', but these are tired clichés best avoided like the plague.

Whatever else it represents, the Burren is an experiment in time travel. What you find there depends on where you look and where you go. It is a rich cosmos, a place that reeks of a deep and enduring history and a charisma of its own. There are many sides to it, with the disciplines of geography, geology, archaeology and botany leading the field. But the Burren, and what it represents, is more than the sum of the many ways in which it can be studied. The spirit of the place eludes some who come in search of it. Others return year after year to their favourite haunts, in favourite seasons, to their likes and dislikes. They have diverse interests, scientific and non-scientific, outdoors and indoors, underground and over ground. But whatever their pursuits, whatever their calling, whatever their dream, they all have one thing in common – an intention to find the spirit of the place and a desire to get drunk on the magic of the unique taste of their own personalised Burren wine. Burrenophilia is not as well known as Francophilia or Anglophilia but is a bona fide philia!

On my annual Burren visits, I have followed one of the Dalai Lama's eighteen Rules for Living: 'Once a year, go somewhere you have never been before.' Frequently, I feel the urgent and disturbing demand of the Burren in my blood. I like the fact that it is a paean to the senses, a hymn to the pleasures of life and a place where you can taste the dynamic quality of nature at first hand. If you desire to know it, feel it and live it, then walk its limestone, sample its silences and light, its uninterrupted horizons, and breathe the elixir of its air. It is an Arcadia, a place you feel at home in after much acclimatising. Everything seems right with the world in this relaxing place. Once the Burren nirvana gets you in its vice-like grip, you are caught.

And always there are the clouds. The English nature writer Enid Wilson once observed: 'Clouds can do strange things in quiet December weather.' In the Burren, this could be applied to the other eleven months as well. Meteorologists have identified at least thirty categories of cloud structure ranging from stratus (near the ground) through altocumulus (medium level) right up to the high cirrus (up to five miles above our heads). Whatever you demand, in terms of shape, size, silhouettes, spectres and suggestions, the Burren clouds offer it.

When you are tired of quartering the ground in your search for gentians, geraniums, mountain avens, ferns, twayblade or early purple orchid, look up and study the cloudscapes. Perhaps you will see them with new eyes and a new inquisitiveness; and as you do, reflect on some lines from Scottish writer Norman MacCaig in his poem 'An Ordinary Day':

> … And my feet took me home
> and my mind observed to me,
> or I to it, how ordinary
> extraordinary things are or
> how extraordinary ordinary
> things are, like the nature of the mind
> and the process of observing.

Afterword

Sarah Poyntz

The people of the Burren coastal villages are people of grit and grace. They bent themselves to survive times that seem, to us today, hard and difficult. When I asked them if their times had been hard they invariably replied, 'They were, but sure we didn't know it and we kept going.' I asked many people if during those hard years they had realised how beautiful the Burren was? I remember the answer of Tom Linnane of Bell Harbour, 'We thought of it as the land God gave us.' His wife, Rena (née Daly) smilingly nodded her head in agreement.

Some said their realisation of the beauty of their surroundings came when visitors and blow-ins were so impressed with it. Their sense of the Burren's loveliness was reinforced when they began to travel around Ireland and abroad.

Indeed the idea of the land's sacredness and beauty were constant themes in oral testimony, in the written word, in the paintings of artists and even in the work of archaeologists.

I think it is true that beauty draws people to it. It has certainly drawn people to live in the Burren. Side by side with the original families are blow-ins from the United States, France, Germany, Italy, the United Kingdom and Brazil, not omitting Irish blow-ins from Wexford (like myself), Wicklow, Limerick, Monaghan, Cork, Dublin and Donegal. There are also regular visitors from all over Europe and America who would never miss their annual stay.

All these very different individuals have, as Fintan O'Toole says in his preface, their very own vision of the Burren, but I think they are all united in the inspiration they draw from the beauty of earth and sky, of hill and ocean, of countryside paths and seaboard walks. In this way, when fog lies on the Burren, rendering all its glory invisible, those who are fortunate to possess a Burren painting by either Manus Walsh, Seamus McGuinness or Denise Ryan can again focus on this rare and powerful loveliness. We can be led to see their vision, to celebrate their joy in nature, to acquiesce in their portrayal of this, our well-beloved landscape.

Contributors

Browne, Pat, is a retired teacher and the son of Primrose (Griffin) and Bill Browne.

Carrucan, Chris and Mick, live in Ballyvaughan. Chris was born there and Mick was born in Fanore. They farm and raise cattle.

Carter, Paul, is a long-time visitor to the Burren, and a keen environmentalist and naturalist. He lives in Bristol.

Clements, Paul, has written two books about Ireland: *Irish Shores, A Journey Round the Rim of Ireland* (1993) and *The Height of Nonsense, The Ultimate Irish Road Trip* (2005). He is a former BBC journalist and a contributing editor to *Insight Guide Ireland* and *Fodor's Ireland*. He is a regular contributor to *The Irish Times* and *Irish Examiner* as well as a range of travel magazines. He teaches creative writing at the Irish Writers' Centre in Dublin and Queen's University in Belfast. A regular visitor to the Burren for twenty years, he holds creative writing workshops in the spring in Ballyvaughan. He is a Fellow of Green College, Oxford.

Comyn, Doreen and Bernie, returned to live on the land of Bernie's ancestors in Ballyvaughan. They are keen on the conservation of the Burren and never prevent people from coming to see their bee orchids on Lough Rask.

Connole, Cathleen (née O'Loughlin), runs 'Burren Fine Wine' in Ballyvaughan.

Cunningham, Carmel, lives and writes in Roscrea. She has been and still is a frequent and loyal visitor to the Burren.

Cunningham, George, was one of the first modern writers on the Burren. His publications include *Burren Journey* (Shannonside, 1978); *Burren Journey West* (Shannonside Tourism, 1980); *Burren Journey North* (Burren Research Press, 1992); *Exploring the Burren* (Town House Country House, 1998); *The Burren Way* – various texts (Shannon Development 1980s–1990s); CD on *Burren Journey West* 2005–2006; Irish Life and Lore Series with Maurice O'Keeffe; and articles in newspapers and magazines on the Burren.

D'Arcy, Gordon, is one of Ireland's leading environmentalists and teaches Irish Studies at the Burren College of Art. He is an authority on the Burren, its wildlife, botany and history and is an artist as well as a writer. His books include *The Natural History of the Burren* and *The Burren Wall*.

Doolan, Lelia, has worked in television, theatre, film and journalism for RTÉ, the Abbey Theatre, the *Irish Press* and many other newspapers and magazines. She spent her childhood summers at her father's home place, Kilshanny, on the edge of the Burren.

Droney, Chris, is a great traditional musician and farmer in Bell Harbour. He is married to Margaret.

Dunford, Brendan *(See O'Connor, Ann)*

Glynn, Liam, lives and works as a GP in Ballyvaughan, County Clare and is a lecturer in Primary Care at the Department of General Practice, NUI Galway.

Gosling, Paul, is an archaeologist who surveyed the archaeological remains on Turlough Hill in the Burren. He lectures and writes, taking a special interest in the Burren in North Clare.

Hartnett, Tony, a Limerick man, is a graphic designer and lives in Bishop's Quarter, Ballyvaughan.

Hawkes-Greene, Mary, is president and a co-founder of the Burren College of Art. She assisted Michael Greene and George Cunningham in establishing the first Burren Spring Conference in 1986.

Hayes, Mary and Christy, live in Ballyvaughan, and are keen conservationists. Christy is retired from the ESB. They grow organic vegetables and fruit, anything from potatoes to grapes.

Hussey, Brian and Anna, began restoring Gregan Castle in 1994, completing the major work in 2002.

Hyland, Jim is a local historian, a retired businessman and hotelier.

Keane, Mary, lives in Lismacteige. She came from Kilshanny and became a farmer's wife on marrying P. J. Keane.

Keane, Maryangela, was one of the first modern writers on the Burren. Her book, *The Burren*, is a classic. She also successfully ran an excellent hotel in Lisdoonvarna with her husband.

Keegan, George, is a bird watcher and he also writes for the *Clare Champion* and *The Irish Times*.

Leonard, John and Sue, are teachers from Plymouth, each with a keen interest in natural history: John (birds) and Sue (flowers). Both have a strong empathy with Ireland and are patrons of the Conservancy of the Burren.

Liberty, Emma Stewart and Wojcik, Paul, rear guide dogs for the blind. In 2009 their bitch produced eleven puppies, bringing the total born in Ballyvaughan to seventy-four.

Longley, Michael, is one of our finest lyric poets. He has a great love for the Burren and has contributed three of his poems inspired by the Burren to this book.

Mahon, Gerard, a farmer and former civil servant, lives with his wife, Madeleine, and family in Ballyvaughan.

Monks, Bernadette and Michael, are former owners of Monks Pub. Although now retired from the hotel business, Michael farms, rearing cattle and winning many prizes. They also keep beautiful little donkeys, rear pigs and keep poultry.

Monks, Fiona, is a qualified veterinarian, now working in Norway after having been an intern at Cambridge University, England.

Moran (née Keane), Breda, commutes between London and Ballyvaughan, where she runs a Bed & Breakfast.

Morton, Jennie, lives in Ballyvaughan with her French husband, Alexis, and two children. She took her degrees at University College Dublin. She is a keen conservationist and grows organic food.

Mulqueeney, Nuala, is the daughter of Micheál Mulqueeney and she carries on her father's tradition in her work at Aillwee Cave.

Nevins Radzinowicz, Mary Ann, lives in Ballyvaughan and was a professor at Vassar College in New York State; Director of Studies in English, Girton College, Cambridge, and Lecturer, University of Cambridge, England; Professor at Cornell University, Ithaca, NY, where she held the Jacob Gould Schurman Chair of English; she is author of *Toward Samson Agonistes* (Princeton University Press, 1978; winner of the Hanford Prize in 1979), *Milton's Epics and the Book of Psalms*, (Princeton University Press, 1989), editor of *American Colonial Prose* (Cambridge University Press, 1984), *Paradise Lost*, Books VII, VIII, eds David Aers, Mary Ann Radzinowicz (Cambridge University Press, 1974; and is an Honoured Scholar of the American Milton Society.

O'Donohue, Brendan, born in Fanore, lives in Ballyvaughan with his wife, Catherine. He is a retired businessman and is a keen environmentalist.

Ó Laighléis, Ré, lives in Ballyvaughan and is a writer of adult, teenage and children's fiction in both English and Irish. His novels and short stories have been widely translated into various languages and he has been the recipient of many literary awards, nationally and internationally. These include Bisto Book of the Year awards, the Oireachtas Literary Award, the North American NAMLLA award, and a European White Ravens Literary Award. In 1998, he was presented with the An Peann faoi Bhláth Award by the president of Ireland, Mary McAleese, in recognition of his contribution to Irish literature. More recently, *An Phleist Mhór*, co-written with Susan Edwards, was adjudged 'Book of the Year for Young Readers' and was awarded the 2008 Réics Carló Award.

O'Connor, Ann and Dunford, Brendan, are the motivators of the Burrenbeo Trust, founded to conserve the Burren.

O'Loughlin, Mortimer, is a local farmer and writes for the *Clare Champion*.

O'Siadhail, Micheal, is one of our foremost poets and scholars. He has published several volumes of poetry and has written *Learning Irish* (Yale University Press, 1995) and *Modern Irish* (Cambridge University Press, 1991). He lectures and reads his poetry worldwide and has received an Irish American Cultural Institute prize for poetry.

O'Toole, Fintan, is a columnist with *The Irish Times*, a critic, biographer, historian and political commentator. His books include *Ship of Fools* (Faber and Faber, London, 2009), *White Savage* (Faber and Faber, London, 2005) and *A Traitor's Kiss* (Granta-Farrar Straus Giroux, London, 1997)

Poyntz, Sarah, was born in New Ross, County Wexford, and was educated in New Ross, in Loreto Abbey, Gorey, and at University College Dublin. She lived for many years in Britain, where she worked as a teacher in Cornwall and Cambridge. She also spent several years in the United States. She first visited the Burren in 1983 and moved to Ballyvaughan village in 1986. She began writing a 'Country Diary' for the *Guardian* newspaper in 1987 and continues to do so. Her collection of these diaries, *A Burren Journal*, was published in 2000. She has also written about growing up in New Ross; some of these works were included in *New Ross, Rosponte, Ros Mhic Treoin: An Anthology Celebrating 800 Years*.

Teskey, Gordon, taught English literature at Cornell University and now teaches at Harvard University. He has made many visits to the Burren villages. His books include *Allegory and Violence* (Cornell University Press, 1996), *The Norton Critical Edition of 'Paradise Lost'* (Norton New York, 2004) and *Delirious Milton* (Harvard University Press, 2006).

Walsh, Justin, is a former pupil of Ballyvaughan National School. He graduated from the NUI Galway with a Bachelor of Arts in Archaeology and History and later with a Master of Arts in History. He trained as a teacher at the University of London's Institute of Education and he is currently teaching history in Parrenthorn High School, a Manchester Secondary School.

Walsh, Manus, is one of Ireland's foremost artists. He lives in Ballyvaughan, paints the Burren, paints in Spain regularly and has painted in Chile.

Ward, Stephen, is a botanist who trained in Wales and Scotland. After a career in nature conservation in Wales, England and

Scotland, he 'retired' to Ballyvaughan, County Clare. He is a director of the Burrenbeo Trust, chair of Clare Biodiversity, joint recorder for County Clare for the Botanical Society of the British Isles and Chair of the United Kingdom-Ireland Limestone Pavement Committee. In his spare time he contributes records for County Clare to the *Bird Atlas 2007–2011*.

Bibliography

Ainsworth, John (ed.), *The Inchiquin Manuscripts* (Stationery Office, Dublin, 1961)

Auden, W. H., *Collected Poems* (Faber and Faber, London, 1976)

Balfe, Michael, *A Burren Village: A Brief History of New Quay and Its Environs* (Frenchman Publications, Bell Harbour, 2006)

Beckett, Samuel, *Watt* (Olympia Press, Paris, 1953, and John Calder, London, 1963)

Betjeman, John, *Ireland With Emily: Collected Poems with Introduction by the Earl of Birkenhead* (Murray, London, 1962)

Breen, Martin, 'A 1570 list of castles in County Clare', *North Munster Antiquarian Journal*, Vol. 36, 1995, pp. 130–38

Breen, Martin and Risteárd Ua Cróinín, 'Towerhouses of the North Burren Coast', *The Other Clare*, Vol. 32, 2008, pp. 5–11

Cabot, David, *Ireland* (Harper Collins, London, 1999)

Cannon, Moya, *Oar* (Salmon Poetry, Co. Clare, 1990)

Clements, Paul, *The Height of Nonsense* (Collins Press, Cork, 2005)

Cooney, Gabriel, *Landscapes of Neolithic Ireland* (Routledge, London, 2000)

Cunningham, George, *Burren Journey* (Shannonside, Shannon, 1978)

Cunningham, George, *Burren Journey West* (Shannonside, Shannon, 1980)

Cunningham, George, *Burren Journey North* (Burren Research Press, Ballyvaughan, 1992)

Cunningham, Melosina Lennox (ed.), *Diaries of Ireland: An Anthology* (Lilliput Press, Dublin, 1998)

D'Arcy, Gordon and Hayward, John, *The Natural History of the Burren* (IMMAL Publishing, London, 1992)

D'Arcy, Gordon, *The Burren Wall* (Tír Eolas, Kinvara, 2006)

Dunford, Brendan, *Farming and the Burren* (Teagasc, Dublin, 2002)

Dunne, Tom (ed.), *New Ross, Rosponte, Ros Mhic Treoin: an anthology celebrating 800 years* (Wexford County Council, 2007)

Frost, James, *The History and Topography of the County of Clare from the Earliest Times to the Beginning of the 18th century* (Sealy, Bryers & Walker, Dublin, 1893)

Gregory, Lady Augusta, 'The Bogie Man', in Saddlemyer, Ann (ed.), *Collected Plays* (Colin Smythe, London, 1971)

Gregory, Lady Augusta, *The Kiltartan Poetry Book* (Putman, London, 1918)

Gosling, Paul, 'Archaeological Implications Report on the Proposed Erection of a "Stone Circle" at the Site of Ballyvaughan Castle, Ballyvaughan, County Clare', unpublished report, Archaeological Services Unit, University College Galway, 1993

Hardiman, James, 'Ancient Irish Deeds and Writings, Chiefly Related to Landed Property, from the Twelfth to the Seventeenth century, with Translations, Notes and a Preliminary Essay', *Transactions of the Royal Academy*, Vol. 15, Antiquities, plus plate, 1828, pp. 2–96

Hogan, Edmund (ed.), *The Description of Ireland and the State thereof as it is at this Present in Anno 1598* (M. H. Gill & Son, Dublin, 1878)

Howard, Ben, *Dark Pool* (Salmon Poetry, County Clare, 2004)

Johnson, Lee, *The Castles of Ireland. Early Stone Fortifications – Castles, Towers and Strong-Houses* (Accessible at: http://www.rootsweb.ancestry.com/-irlkik/ihm/castles/ircastl-Clare.htm, accessed 4 April, 2009)

Jones, Carleton, *The Burren and the Aran Islands: Exploring the Archaeology* (Collins Press, Cork, 2004)

Keane, Maryangela, *The Burren* (Irish Heritage 30, Eason, Dublin, 1983)

Keating, Geoffrey, *The History of Ireland: Foras Feasa ar Éirinn*, trans. O'Mahony, 3 vols (Irish Genealogical Foundation, Dublin, 1980)

Kee, Robert, *The Green Flag, Volume 1–3: The Most Distressful Country, The Bold Fenian Men, Ourselves Alone* (Penguin, London, 2000)

Kickham, Charles J., *Knocknagow* (Gill, Dublin, 1962)

Kilroe, J. R., *A Description of the Soil-Geology of Ireland* (His Majesty's Stationery Office, Dublin, 1907)

Lawless, Emily, *Hurrish* (Nelson, London, 1886)

Leask, Harold, *Irish Castles and Crenellated Houses* (Dundalk, revised 2nd edn, 1951)

Lennon, Colm, *Sixteenth-century Ireland. The Incomplete Conquest* (revised edn, Gill & Macmillan, Dublin, 2005)

Le Roy, Ladurie, *Montaillou* (Editions Gallimard, 1978)

Longley, Michael, *Collected Poems* (Jonathan Cape, London, 2006)

Ludlow, Edmund, *The Memoirs of Edmund Ludlow*, edited by C. H. Firth (Clarendon Press, Oxford, 1894)

Mabey, Richard and Tony Evans, *The Flowering of Britain* (Arrow Books, London, 1980)

MacCaig, Norman, *Collected Poems* (Chatto and Windus, London, 1990)

Mac Cárthaigh, Criostóir (ed.), *The Traditional Boats of Ireland* (Collins Press, Cork, 2008)

Mackenzie, Murdoch, *A Maritime Survey of Ireland and the West of Great Britain; Taken by the Order of the Right Honourable the Lords Commissioners of Admiralty; in Two Volumes Accompanied with a Book of Nautical Descriptions and Directions to each volume*, 2 vols (privately published by Murdoch Mackenzie, London, 1776)

Mapother, Edward Dillon, *The Treatment of Chronic Skin Diseases, with an Appendix of Lisdoonvarna Spas and Seaside Places of Clare* (Fannin, Dublin, 1872)

McNeill, Tom, *Castles in Ireland. Feudal power in a Gaelic world* (Routledge, London, 1997)

Moore, George, *Ave* (Heinemann, London, 1947)

Nelson, Charles and Wendy Walsh, *The Burren: A companion to the Wildflowers of an Irish Limestone Wilderness* (Boethius Press & The Conservancy of the Burren, 1991)

O'Connell, Gerald (ed.), *The Burren: a guide* (Limerick, 1973)

O'Connell, J. W. and A. Korrf (eds), *The Book of the Burren* (Tír Eolas, Kinvara, 1991)

Ó Dálaigh, Brian, Breen, Martin and Ristéard Ua Cróinín, 'The Edenvale Castle Survey of Co. Clare 1671–79', *The North Munster Antiquarian Journal*, Vol. 45, 2005, pp. 33–47

O'Donoghue, John, *Echoes of Memory* (Salmon, 1994; Transworld/Random House, 2009)

O'Donoghue, John, *Anam Cara* (Bantam, London, 1997)

O'Donoghue, John, *Eternal Echoes* (Bantam, London, 1998)

O'Donoghue, John, *Conamara Blues* (Transworld/Doubleday, 2000)

O'Donoghue, John, *Divine Beauty* (Bantam, London, 2003)

O'Donoghue, John, *Benedictus* (Bantam, London, 2007)

O'Donohue, Tony, *Front Row Center* (Abbeyfield Publishers, Toronto, Canada, 2001)

O'Donovan, John (ed.), *Annals of the Kingdom of Ireland, by the Four Masters, from the Earliest Period to the year 1616*, 7 vols (Hodges, Smith and Co., Dublin, 1854)

O'Flanagan, M. (ed.), 'Letters containing information relative to the antiquities of the county of Clare collected during the progress of the Ordnance Survey in 1839', Vol. 1, unpublished typescript, Bray, 1928

Ó Ruairc, Pádraig Óg, *Blood on the Banner* (Mercier Press, Cork, 2009)

Poyntz, Sarah, *A Burren Journal* (Tír Eolas, Kinvara, 2000)

Plunkett, James, *The Gems She Wore* (Hutchinson, London, 1972)

Praeger, Robert Lloyd, *The Way that I Went* (Collins Press, Cork, 1997; first published Hodges Figgis, Dublin, 1937)

Robinson, Tim, *Stones of Aran: Pilgrimage* (Lilliput in association with Wolfhound Press, Dublin, 1986)

Robinson, Tim, *Stones of Aran: Labyrinth* (Lilliput, Dublin, 1995)

Robinson, Tim, *The Burren* (Folding Landscapes, Roundstone, 1999)

Simms, Mike, *Exploring the Limestone Landscapes of the Burren and the Gort Lowlands* (Burrenkarst, Belfast, 2001)

Spenser, Edmund, *The Faerie Queen* (edited by A. C. Hamilton; Longman, London, 1997)

Solnit, Rebecca, *A Book of Migrations: Some Passages in Ireland* (Verso, London, 1997)

Swinfen, Averil, *Forgotten Stones* (Lilliput, Dublin, 1992)

Synge, John Millington, *The Aran Islands* (Oxford University Press, London, 1962)

Tratman, E. K. (ed.), *The Caves of North-West Clare, Ireland* (David and Charles, Newton Abbot, 1969)

Twigge, R. W., 'Edward White's Description of Thomond in 1574', *Journal of the North Munster Archaeological Society*, Vol. 1, no. 2, 1909, pp. 75–85

Viney, Michael, *Ireland* (Blackstaff Press, Belfast, 2003)

Viney, Michael and Ethna, *Ireland's Ocean* (Collins Press, Cork, 2008)

Walters, Brian, *Fallen: My Travels in Ireland and Eastern Europe* (Virtualbookworm.com Publishing, 2004)

Westropp, Thomas J., 'Notes on the Lesser Castles or "Peel Towers" of the County Clare', *Proceedings of the Royal Irish Academy*, 3rd series, Vol. 5 (1899), pp. 348–65

Westropp, Thomas J., 'Descriptive Account of the Places Visited on the Summer Excursion of the Royal Society of Antiquaries of Ireland, 1900', *Journal of the Royal Society of Antiquaries of Ireland*, Vol. 30, pp. 273–306

Westropp, Thomas J., 'Prehistoric Remains of North-Western Clare', *Journal of the Royal Society of Antiquaries of Ireland*, Vol. 31 (1901), pp. 273–92

White, Patrick, *History of Clare and the Dalcassian Clans* (M. H. Gill & Sons, Dublin, 1893)

Wilson, David A., *Ireland, a Bicycle and a Tin Whistle* (Blackstaff, Belfast, 1995)

Wilson, Enid, *Enid Wilson's Country Diaries* (Hodder and Stoughton, London, 1990)

Wordsworth, William, *The Poetical Works* (Nimmo, Hay & Mitchell, Edinburgh, 1900)

Yeats, W. B., 'The Dreaming of the Bones', in *Collected Plays* (Macmillan, London, 1953)

Yeats, W. B., *Ireland and the Arts, Essays and Introductions* (Macmillan, London, 1961)

Acknowledgements

Every step of the way they stood by me: my friend Mary Ann Nevins Radzinowicz with her daily encouragement; her son, Bill or Liam, and her daughter, Annie, with professional advice; my dear friends Helen and Brendan Monks, who loaned books, gave maps, information and guidance; my loyal friend Margie Kirk of Stratford-on-Avon with her support. Jennie Morton's help was indispensable. The Clare Local Studies Centre (Peter and Brian) gave me invaluable assistance. The idea for this book originated when Dr Ronan Kavanagh gave me *The Last of the Name*, being the memories of Charles McGlinchey (as told to Ronan's grandfather, Patrick, and written up by his father, Des) and from a meeting with Mary Hayes by the sea front in Ballyvaughan when we chatted about her husband Christy's wonderful stories. My sincere thanks to them and to all the people of the coastal villages who helped with information; to those who contributed their prose or poetry; to the business proprietors and post offices for putting notices in their premises; and to Fr Forde for his Sunday announcements; to Micheal O'Siadhail for his poem 'Vocation', written specially for this book; and to Michael Longley for his poems. Anna and Brian Hussey were most supportive. Marie Greene, Deirdre Hyland, Dympna Hyland and Mary Keegan encouraged me throughout. I am indebted to Christine O'Connor, Fanore, for the loan of the CD made by the late John McNamara of her late father's memories of his fishing days off Gleninagh; to Con Collins of the Collins Press, Cork, for permission to use references and information from the magnificent *Traditional Boats of Ireland: History, Folklore and Construction*, edited by Criostóir Mac Cárthaigh; to Tony and Brendan O'Donohue for permission to use material on Fanore from *Front Row Center, A Perspective on Life, Politics and the Environment*; to Tomás Mac Conmara, project manager, and Darina Tully, Clare Traditional Boats and Currachs Study, for permission to use material from their project; to Mr John Cudlipp, chairman, Eason & Son Ltd, for permission to use material from their publication *The Martello Towers of Ireland* by Victor J. Enoch; and to all who supplied photos – to Redmonds of Roscrea and especially to Karen Funke.

My sincere thanks to all the team at the Mercier Press for their unfailing patience and professional expertise.

The community appreciates the donation of land for leisure purposes by Mr Paddy Kerins (bird hide) and by the Clancy and O'Donohue families (walking path).

The Burren Code

Please do not disturb the limestone pavement
Preserve natural habitats
Please do not pick wild flowers, plants, shrubs
Do not damage walls, buildings, monuments
Respect landowners, their property, their animals
Park and camp in designated areas
Take away nothing but memories and photos